Women and the Bible

Contents

The Hebrew Aleph Bet   2

Introduction   4

Chapter 1   6
Part 1 The Join   6
Part 2 Prophesy   22
Part 3 Take cover   35

Chapter 2   43
God's Opinion

Chapter 3   73
Truth

Chapter 4   79
Women A

Chapter 5   95
Women Bee

Chapter 6   102
Therefore

The Hebrew Aleph Bet
Words receive meaning derived from the combined meaning of their letters.

ALEPH			OX	Ox, first, leader, aloof, strong
BETH			HOUSE	Household, house, into, in, family, inside
GIMEL			CAMEL	Reward, exultation, lift up, pride, benefit
DALET			DOOR	Door, path, entrance
HEY			BEHOLD	Behold, reveal, 'the'
WAW			NAIL	Hook, nail, secure, add, 'and'
ZAYIN			WEAPON	Weapon, cut, cut off
CHET			FENCE	Fence, separate, private
TET			SURROUND	Surround
YOOD			HAND	Make, hand, work, deed
KAF			PALM	Palm, cover, open, allow
LAMED			STAFF	Authority, the tongue, guide, control
MEM			WATER	Life, water, massive, chaos
NOON			LIFE	Activity, fish, action, lively
SAMECH			PROP	Prop, support, turn
AYIN			EYE	Know, experience, see, eye
PEY			MOUTH	Speak, a word, mouth, voice, open
TSADE			FISH HOOK	Need, hook, catch, desire
QOOF			BACK OF THE HEAD	Last, least, behind
REYSH			HEAD	Head, person, highest
SHEEN			TEETH	Teeth, destroy, devour, consume
TAV			SIGN	The sign, a covenant, a seal, the cross

Introduction

To everyone running to and fro looking for something to believe in. In search of the account of events for this planet. So many of us are busy doing God knows what, looking under every leaf and tree to find the meaning of life. Through a seamless course of events, historical accounts have taught us that religious wars, dissensions, disagreements, genocides and cataclysmic phenomenon are the fault of God.

However, according to Napoleon Bonaparte 'history is a set of lies agreed upon'.

There is no creator, there cannot be. No. Why would such a God allow so much suffering in the world? And anyway, all those fanciful tales of apples and gardens of Eden, worldwide floods and walking on water. Come on, be serious this is the real suited-and-booted-got-to-get-up-to-go-to-work-in-the-morning world.

Meanwhile all births, marriages and deaths occur with the involvement of this God. Those who classify themselves as 'gay' want to be married with his permission. Every court of law in the world waits upon the swearing, one way or another, of truth bound by this God, given by all who speak therein. If he were real, then he would speak to all of us. We would have seen him if he were real. And how about all those people in India who will never know about him? What happens to them? All those innocent people can't go to hell when they die. No caring god would do that. Anyway, where is this hell? It's all a twisted myth, conjured up by modern society to opiate the masses. It's always some lofty pious rich religious guy from on high telling the proletariat what to do, what not to do and how much to pay him.

I never have spent one minute in any seminary, bible school or any other place of learning that professes to raise a man up to the position where he qualifies to be the mouth of God on earth. However, that same God these experts, clergy, preachers, popes, pastors and deacons all appear to be talking about talks to me every day. In fact sometimes He talks so much that I have to get a piece of paper and a pen out to keep up with what He is saying.

I am forty-six years old now and He has been yabbering in my ears for more than forty-six years.

I would say, about 0.3 percent of the stuff I have heard from these 'experts' on God is true (0.3 because it is certainly less than once in every 200 comments).

Nope, I haven't had one good God damn day of seminary/cemetery teaching and I think I am doing okay. Listening to Him, chatting to Him and making sense of my life in general. As a Koran reader would say, I am one of the 'people of the Book'. So being a nobody in the grand seminary/cemetery scheme of things, may I invite you to dive into the scriptures with me and discover what this 'God' is really saying to women?

Okay, let's go.

Chapter 1

Part 1   The Join

1 Corinthians 7:1

"Now concerning the things whereof ye wrote unto me: It is good for a man not to touch[680] a woman."
Paul says that it is 'good' not to be attached. 680 in the Strong's New Testament dictionary is the Greek word 'haptomai', defined in English as 'attach oneself to'. Paul reckons it is good not to have 'another half', as we say in worldly terminology.
He thinks that marriage is not a matter to enter into lightly. If you intend to enter in lightly, then it is best for you not to enter in at all. Marriage is to be a serious attachment. You are now connected and after the marriage rite, like a new creation you two literally move as one. Indeed as full of glory as the new creation of salvation, 2 Timothy 2:10 and Hebrews 2:10. Marriage is resolute. God wants to do something with the couple as one singular powerful entity, Ephesians 5:30-33;
"For we are members of his body, of his flesh, and of his bones. For this cause shall a man leave his father and mother, and shall be joined unto his wife, and they two shall be one flesh. This is a great mystery: but I speak concerning Christ and the church. Nevertheless let every one of you in particular so love his wife even as himself; and the wife see that she reverence her husband."

Marriage is a great mystery says Paul; a great God given opportunity of corporate glory and enigma. Also note that it is the man who leaves his ancestral line to Join the woman's. This is a matriarchal precedent whereby cultural identity is handed down through the woman. This is a little spoken of foundational premise of Hebrew culture and you only qualify as Hebrew if your mother, not your father, is Hebrew. However, later we will address how largely men (see Malachi 2) are misplacing the opportunity of glory within the family unit.
Paul says it is a mystery, and no, he is not talking about the Church and Christ in this instance. How could he say Christ and the Church are a great mystery when he himself has been commissioned to unravel the truth of the scriptures to us? Ephesians 3:8-10;

"Unto me, who am less than the least of all saints, is this grace given, that I should preach among the Gentiles the unsearchable riches of Christ; And to make all men see what is the fellowship of the mystery, which from the beginning of the world hath been hid in God, who created all things by Jesus Christ: To the intent that now unto the principalities and powers in heavenly places might be known by the church the manifold wisdom of God,.."

No, he is not a double minded character; he speaks of man and woman in marriage being a mystery.

I would like to change the etymology of 'marriage' here into the word 'Join'. I will capitalize it to try to ensure its distinction from the word 'join' if I use it. So when you see the word 'Join', read 'marriage' and comprehend better its meaning.

Paul says that he speaks concerning Christ and the Church. What he means is that he is primarily gifted to expound upon and deliver information regarding Jesus Christ and the Church – that it his ministry and his calling. He is saying that talking about men and women Joined together is not his express gifting.

When you read the bible, you have to do so as though you were reading a piece of Shakespeare, Steinbeck or Orwell etc, to revise for your English Literature examination. Don't just gloss over sentences or phrases that do not seem to fit with the rest of the discourse. They do. You just need to wait a while, add a little wisdom and let the scripture go deeper and explain itself. Paul doesn't know what the great mystery in the Joining of a man and a woman is. He is not Joined himself and says in 1 Corinthians 7:7-9;

"For I would that all men were even as I myself. But every man hath his proper gift of God, one after this manner, and another after that. I say therefore to the unmarried and widows, it is good for them if they abide even as I. But if they cannot contain, let them marry: for it is better to marry than to burn."

(By the way, I don't think he means burn as in 'hell fire' here. He just means the suppression of sexual energy.)

He is not Joined himself, and so is not in authority to talk about what this mystery is; he just knows that there is one. He says in Ephesians 5:33;

"Nevertheless let every one of you in particular so love his wife even as himself; and the wife see that she reverence her husband."

He is clearly telling us that he is doing his best to deliver some helpful guidance for husbands and wives in order to restore some balance that may have been lacking thereof in the early Church.

But the reader must be aware; he is not going to deliver any revelation regarding Joining. He is not an expert on the issue, he can only help those in a Join to stay afloat, i.e., to 'tread water' so to speak and maintain what they have already received. 1 Corinthians 7:1;

"...It is good for a man not to touch a woman."

Well this is his own opinion, being a single man. It is not God's, Proverbs 18:22;

"Whoso findeth a wife findeth a good thing, and obtaineth favour of the Lord."

Paul goes on to say in 1 Corinthians 7:6;

"But I speak this by permission, and not of commandment."

The fact he is clearly stating the advice he is offering is not law tells us that his help is for those who have not yet gone deep enough into God to elicit help for themselves. This is further demonstrated in verse 12 where he says;

"But to the rest speak I, not the Lord: If any brother hath a wife that believeth not, and she be pleased to dwell with him, let him not put her away."

Now, let's imagine him saying '...speak I, not the Lord about the Love of God...' we would all wonder why he was bothering to speak.

So, regarding the above scripture, he is basically saying that he is just trying to help. Paul is a man that seeks God on all of the issues he teaches. Yet, this issue is not one for which God has delivered *revelation* to him. God has not delivered revelation to him on this issue because God has told him that it is a mystery. That does not mean that God tells every believer that Joining is a mystery. God is no respecter of persons and when He is ready to tell anybody something, He will. If that person does not receive the information, listen and act accordingly, He will go ahead and get a donkey to speak, or wait for a rock to cry out. Call me donkey rock.

Verse 6;

"But I speak this by permission[4774], and not of commandment."

4774 in Strong's for the Greek language is 'suggnómé', by definition, 'indulgence, concession'. I.e., Paul is saying, 'If you have heard a personal revelation from God on this issue, chuck everything I have just said in the bin.'

Now in view of the fact that not only is the New Testament telling us (let us use the words 'new contract' from here on to represent in modern etymology the words 'New Covenant' which the New Testament is) that the letter of the law has died, Paul is further reducting to documenting his 'permission'.

We are not bound by rules and regulation in God's new contract to us, Galatians 3:17-28;

"And this I say, that the covenant, that was confirmed before of God in Christ, the law, which was four hundred and thirty years after, cannot disannul, that it should make the promise of none effect. For if the inheritance be of the law, it is no more of promise: but God gave it to Abraham by promise. Wherefore then serveth the law? It was added because of transgressions, till the seed should come to whom the promise was made... If there had been a law given which could have given life, verily righteousness should have been by the law... before faith came, we were kept under the law, shut up unto the faith which should afterwards be revealed. Wherefore the law was our schoolmaster to bring us unto Christ, that we might be justified by faith. But after that faith is come, we are no longer under a schoolmaster. For ye are all the children of God by faith in Christ Jesus. For as many of you as have been baptized into Christ have put on Christ. There is neither Jew nor Greek, there is neither bond nor free, there is neither male nor female: for ye are all one in Christ Jesus."

Hello everybody. Wake up. Paul talks on general maintenance of a Join. There is no revelatory information regarding a Join here, no instructions on its higher eternal performance to take note of.

Paul's permission is subordinate to the law, the law is subordinate to Love; Love is the whole of the new contract. Mark 12:29-34;

"And Jesus answered him, 'The first of all the commandments is, Hear, O Israel; The Lord our God is one Lord: And thou shalt love the Lord thy God with all thy heart, and with all thy soul, and with all thy mind, and with all thy strength: this is the first commandment. And the second is like, namely this, Thou shalt love thy neighbour as thyself. There is none other commandment greater than these.' And the scribe said unto him, Well, Master, thou hast said the truth: for there is one God; and there is none other but he: And to love him with all the heart, and with all the understanding, and with all the soul, and with all the strength, and to love his neighbour as himself, is more than all whole burnt

offerings and sacrifices. And when Jesus saw that he answered discreetly, he said unto him, 'Thou art not far from the kingdom of God.' And no man after that durst ask him any question."

When the husband loves God completely hook line and sinker and the wife loves God completely hook line and sinker, they automatically love themselves. When they love their spouse as their own self, then that is the whole ticket, no arguing, no divorce, struggle over.

Galatians 5:14;
"For all the law is fulfilled in one word, even in this; Thou shalt love thy neighbour as thyself."
1 John 4:16-17;
"And we have known and believed the love that God hath to us. God is love; and he that dwelleth in love dwelleth in God, and God in him. Herein is our love made perfect, that we may have boldness in the day of judgment: because as he is, so are we in this world."

So let us wake up to boldness, let us wake up to being Him in this place, let us wake up to the real energy of Love. Every Join is different and every Join must be based in its own original flavour, history and splendour. It is time that all of us in the Body gained a good concrete understanding of just what this thing, paralleled with Christ's relationship with His church, has the Almighty power to do in this earth.
Like the man John Coltrane, blow a love supreme.

Paul goes on to give further help. 1 Corinthians 7:3;
"Let the husband render unto the wife due benevolence[2133]: and likewise also the wife unto the husband."
If the husband is always the first to move in kindness, a Godly Join will have no lasting problems. This is one of the best messages of help that Paul gives on this subject. 2133, 'eunoia' is defined as 'kindness, goodwill'. The husband is expected to be kind to the wife; this is the beginning. Then 'likewise' the wife to the husband.

7:4
"The wife hath not power[1850] of her own body, but the husband: and likewise also the husband hath not power[1850] of his own body but the wife."

1850 in Strong's Greek translation is 'exousiazo', defined as to 'exercise authority on'. Each is capable of changing the mood and state of the other for good or for bad. So choose the good.

It must be stressed here that though maintenance, the message of due benevolence is a very important message from Paul. Due benevolence is not meant to be given to your spouse in a spirit of a compromise orientated move away from God; "Oh okay then, although I am dying inside". The word of God here is very clear that at the base of the Join there is to be due benevolence; kindness and goodwill that is not just an abstract act. It is naturally due to the one you love.

This 'due' benevolence is what, when the Join began, was due from each person to the other. For example, a woman who loves her husband is not going to sulk if he doesn't do the washing up one night and let due kindness and goodwill towards him slip away. Rather, a deep seated lack of assistance or respect for the other spouse suddenly or slowly creeping in could result in non-benevolence. Both in the Join will sense its presence. They may sense it based on hurt feelings or based on the guilt of instigating it. Whoever may be responsible for that lack of benevolence should not disrespect that union by expecting the other to move further away from God, in order to stand parallel with them. This courts bad behaviour or at best bad will by means of reciprocation. That is not benevolence one to the other. It ushers in ungodliness and compromise. This frustrates man's spiritual stability and can ultimately frustrate the grace of God.

Benevolence cannot be expected by the husband from his wife if there is not continual and untarnished love going from him to her. Then likewise, love goes from her to him. If the husband is negating the worth of the wife through aggression or disrespect, he is disrespecting the Join and so disrespecting himself and should repent. If she has anything to repent over, it will happen naturally when his negativity has ceased and he purposefully moves in love towards her.

When one or both repent, they should make quality decisions not to perform in that way towards the other again.

There is the word repent found in 2 Corinthians 7:8 which is also what Judas did in Matthew 27:3, Strong's number 3338 'metamellomai' defined as 'to care afterwards', or regret and repent to yourself.
No. Not that.

I am talking about repent found in Revelations 2:5 or Acts 17:30, 3340 'metanoeo', 'to think differently'.

To my knowledge if you want to remove an undesirable fruit tree you remove its one root ball. A problem always has a root, and in a Join it can be located back to one point. I have never heard of a situation where a problem was caused by both parties simultaneously doing something. The guilty party should come clean or if they are not aware of how they have caused hurt, enquire as to why the other party feels benevolence is not due to them. If one withholds benevolence it is usually either due to the other (in which case that original root of non-benevolence needs to be uprooted) or due to some outside party's influence (in which case it needs to be exposed, addressed and rooted out). The bible says in Ephesians 5:31 and Matthew 19:6 that;
"For this cause shall a man leave his father and mother, and shall be joined unto his wife, and they two shall be one flesh."
" 'Wherefore they are no more twain, but one flesh. What therefore God hath joined together, let not man put asunder.' "
By the way, Jesus does not say that God may not make an end to it. He is sovereign and if one of His children, being Joined, is suffering to the point where their salvation or the salvation of their children is becoming unstable He will do as He sees fit. Those parties hearing Him on the issue had better proceed accordingly.

Whatever may be festering in one spouse is also trying its best to fester in the other. That whatever needs to be stamped out, killed and composted for the sake of good news. God puts two together to help bring Jesus Christ back, not to hinder. A festering phunk in a Join is an onerous odour to God and He must look the other way as concerns any good calling for those harbouring such a thing.

The bible says in Malachi 2:8-16 speaking of men in a Join;
"But ye are departed out of the way; ye have caused many to stumble at the law; ye have corrupted the covenant of Levi, saith the Lord of hosts. Therefore have I also made you contemptible and base before all the people, according as ye have not kept my ways, but have been partial in the law. Have we not all one father? hath not one God created us? why do we deal treacherously every man against his brother[251], by profaning the covenant of our fathers? Judah hath dealt treacherously, and an abomination is committed in Israel and in Jerusalem; for Judah hath profaned the

12

holiness of the Lord which he loved, and hath married the daughter of a strange god. The Lord will cut off the man that doeth this, the master and the scholar, out of the tabernacle of Jacob, and him that offereth an offering unto the Lord of hosts. And this ye have done again, covering the altar of the Lord with tears, weeping, and with crying out, insomuch that he regardeth not the offering anymore, or receiveth with good will at your hand. Yet ye say, Wherefore? Because the Lord hath been witness between thee and the wife of thy youth, against whom thou hast dealt treacherously: yet she thy companion, and the wife of thy covenant. And did not He make one? Yet had he the residue[7605](7605 'shar'; rest, residue, remnant, remainder) of the spirit. And wherefore one? That He might seek a Godly[430](430 'elhym'; plural-, to act as divine rulers or judges) seed[2233](2233 'zru'; singular-, sowing, crop, offspring; as a singular meaning). Therefore take heed to your spirit, and let none deal treacherously against the wife of his youth. For the Lord, the God of Israel, saith that he hateth putting away: for one covereth violence with his garment, saith the Lord of hosts: therefore take heed to your spirit, that ye deal not treacherously."

All of that mess, based on men behaving badly.

Firstly, let me address the fact that we have men behaving badly today yes we do. In the above text the word brother is given the Strong's Hebrew dictionary number 251 'ach', Aleph, Chet, in the Hebrew language, 'brother'. However the actual word used in the original Hebrew text is 'bachhwv', Bet, Aleph, Chet, Hey, Wav; 'Into the first separated revealed security'. This has the more appropriate definition of 'over or upon another of your kinsman/relatives', i.e., not exclusively a brother. So therefore the whole discourse above regarding how fed up God is with men pertains to how fed up God is with Hebrew men behaving badly towards their Hebrew wives. Malachi goes on to quote God Himself in 4:5-6 saying;

"Behold, I will send you Elijah the prophet before the coming of the great and dreadful day of the Lord: And he shall turn the heart of the fathers[1] to the children, and the heart of the children to their fathers[1], lest I come and smite the earth with a curse."

Interestingly, that is the last verse of the Old Testament so we do well to pay attention to the fine detail. Strong's number 1 is used for the word 'fathers'; Aleph, Bet, 'av' or 'ab' in Hebrew. However, the word in the original scripture is not that. It is actually Aleph, Bet, Wav, Chet, in the first occurrence above and Aleph, Bet, Wav, Chet, Mem in the second; 'abwvch' and 'abwvchm' respectively. These would be more satisfactorily translated as 'Hebrew households' and 'Ancestral Hebrew households'; 'The first households secured by separation', and 'The first households secured by separation as massive'.

This means that God is saying He needs Hebrew men and women Joined together in harmonic family groups, before Jesus can come back again for the final judgement.

If we do not get this right, and the original, real Hebrew men do not wake up, stop going after other women and foolishness and turn back to their wives God gave them, then God will turn this whole place into a curse. But that's okay. Because men are destined to straighten up and fly right.

I need to make a book specifically for the brothers. If the subject is not exhausted by the end of this one.

God is speaking through the prophet Malachi to males. Malachi asserts that the males have the rest 'residue' of the spirit necessary to enable Christ to come. This is their seed that they combined in their wives' wombs to keep the generations going in order to see the first appearance of Jesus via his mother Mary. So, the males/husbands have the rest of the anointing/spirit. We ladies have the bulk of that anointing being the vessels with wombs. This means that God actually requires us, the paired male and female, to get it done in the earth. Making two into one is God's perfect method for the development of a strong team and a holy nation. The development of this teamwork was how God managed to get Jesus here the first time. We also need it to get Him back the second time with faith that evolves into knowing, 2 Timothy 1:12;

"I know whom I have believed."

and in working that knowledge together the husband and wife team can prophesy and therefore bring about team 'return of Jesus Christ'.

The 'seed' ultimately is Christ Jesus. Those were the days of Malachi. They managed to get past their problems and enough prophecy and right living was engaged in to bring in motion the birth of Jesus.

Now in the body of Christ and after His first coming, we are called to usher in His second coming. How much more do we in these latter days need to align ourselves together as married couples against worldly foolishness? Let's get it right with our husbands in order to prophesy for the fulfilment of His word so Jesus can take His heavenly slippers off, fold up His dressing gown and come back here.

Malachi was not just talking about Jesus coming the first time because we can see below that he mentions forms of judgement, which are yet to come, Malachi 3:2-6;

"But who may abide the day of his coming? and who shall stand when he appeareth? for he is like a refiner's fire, and like fullers' soap: And he shall sit as a refiner and purifier of silver: and he shall purify the sons of Levi, and purge them as gold and silver, that they may offer unto the Lord an offering in righteousness. Then shall the offering of Judah and Jerusalem be pleasant unto the Lord, as in the days of old, and as in former years. And I will come near to you to judgment; and I will be a swift witness against the sorcerers, and against the adulterers, and against false swearers, and against those that oppress the hireling in his wages, the widow, and the fatherless, and that turn aside the stranger from his right, and fear not me, saith the Lord of hosts. For I am the Lord, I change not; therefore ye sons of Jacob are not consumed."

Boy, do we need a swift witness against all abhorrent secret societies and official liars today.

God will always hold the head of the Join responsible for the outcome of a Join. It is time for us all to stop being nice and pretending. It is usually men that sour a good relationship. So it is time to repair the breach and restore the paths so everyone can dwell in peace and safety. Get back in love with God's chosen one for you, and get it on. 1 Corinthians 7:5 **"Defraud ye not one the other, except with consent for a time that ye may give yourselves to fasting and prayer; and come together again, that satan tempt you not for your incontinency[192]."**

192 is 'akrasia', 'lack of self restraint'. Paul says he speaks by permission. As previously mentioned, he means that this is not a commandment from God, but guidelines he needs to give according to his personal observations. Really, I take it that all of what he says about a Join, not being privy to the mystery himself, are general guidelines to be taken on if you have not received superior information from the throne room. And God is not silly. Those superior instructions will be of best and lasting benefit to all involved. And it will be obvious to all involved because He is God. So there is nowhere to hide from a bad decision, pretending to be super spiritual, and then blaming it on God.

In particular, sex is a very personal physical thing where a soul can be tormented as a result of taking part in it, if the other party is not right with God. We all need to move continually towards God. God speaks to all of us as clear unique individuals in every situation. In verse 12 Paul says;

"But to the rest[3062] speak I, not the Lord:…"

Speaking of the 'rest', Strong's 3062, 'loipos', defined as 'the remaining', Paul is talking about other circumstances which may court advice within the Join.

Each Join is a different living entity and one living being. Don't kill it, don't squash it and don't force it into a uniform mould. Give it every chance to live and breathe with its own uniqueness.

Paul then gives instruction on what he thinks is appropriate in general situations which we shall look into later. First though, a directive from God;

7:10-11

"And unto the married I command, not I, but the Lord, Let not the wife depart from husband: But and if she depart let her remain unmarried, or be reconciled[2644] to husband; and let not the husband put away wife."

2644 is 'katallasso', which is defined as, 'to change mutually'.

It is clear what Paul is saying here; about to deal with an unbeliever in a Join, he is now dealing with a believing couple.

A simple explanation from me. If you two got married as grown up believing God loving adults, and are still both grown up believing God loving adults then, stay the hell together and stop talking nonsense about splitting up. However if one (or both) of you have lost the faith, or one (or both) have lost the faith and are pretending to still have it, then you both will know. If you are the believing party, get the hell out of it. 2 Corinthians 6:14-17;

"Be ye not unequally yoked together with unbelievers: for what fellowship hath righteousness with unrighteousness? and what communion hath light with darkness? And what concord hath Christ with Belial? or what part hath he that believeth with an infidel? And what agreement hath the temple of God with idols? for ye are the temple of the living God; as God hath said, I will dwell in them, and walk in them; and I will be their God, and they shall be my people. Wherefore come out from among them, and be ye separate, saith the Lord, and touch not the unclean thing; and I will receive you."

Get out before your rear end gets burned.

It is worse for the unbeliever who once 'believed'. Mark 3:29, Hebrews 10:38-39;

" 'But he that shall blaspheme against the Holy Ghost hath never forgiveness, but is in danger of eternal damnation.' "

"Now the just shall live by faith: but if any man draw back, my soul shall have no pleasure in him. But we are not of them who draw back unto perdition; but of them that believe to the saving of the soul."

Your only problem, as the one in the Join who still believes, is to walk that tricky path of condemnation from the pretender and from the 'church goers' who wouldn't know the truth from the sole of Dangermouse's foot.

Paul says in 1Corinthians 7:10 that this is a command not from himself but from the Lord. He says the two should not split up but if they do they should come back together after changing mutually. Obviously that change should be toward God. No party should be put in a position to compromise their faith in a step away from the will of God. This is obvious. The word reconciled in translation means mutual change. This is because after the disagreement, one (or both) must forgive and forget after the other (or both) have moved on and changed mutually toward the truth. That is the only way forgiveness can happen when you are Joined to another. In other circumstances we forgive because we know that God is our source and we respect none but Him to butter our bread. However, in the marvellous 'mystery' of the Join, we are one. There is nowhere to hide and if part of you has done something wrong then you know that y'all need to change.

All of this advice is still of maintenance in nature, we have not gone deep yet,

"Deep calleth unto deep at the noise of thy waterspouts…"

Our man David in the above scripture Psalm 42:7, knows something about the dynamics of love. There is no unfolding or development of the mystery of the Join in Paul's delivery, so don't hold your breath for it.

In 1 Corinthians 7:12-17 Paul goes on to talk in his own strength;

"But to the rest speak I, not the Lord: If any brother hath a wife that believeth not, and she be pleased to dwell with him, let him not put her away. And the woman which hath an husband that

believeth not, and if he be pleased to dwell with her, let her not leave him. For the unbelieving husband is sanctified by the wife, and the unbelieving wife is sanctified by the husband: else were your children unclean; but now are they holy. But if the unbelieving depart, let him depart. A brother or a sister is not under bondage in such: but God hath called us to peace[1515](1515, 'eirene', to join, rest, set at one again). For what knowest thou, O wife, whether thou shalt save husband? or how knowest thou, O man, whether thou shalt save wife? But as God hath distributed to every man, as the Lord hath called every one, so let him walk..."

Thank you Paul, good clear common sense.

He then goes on to speak about the situation for virgins following this statement in 1 Corinthians 7:27;
"Art thou bound unto a wife? seek not to be loosed. Art thou loosed from a wife? seek not a wife."
Erm, Paul, 'bound'? Loosed? Poor baby. What horrible wife have you experienced?
Now Paul had a very colourful past. So colourful that God had to intervene and stop him on his path before he did serious damage to the early Church. I imagine, when I think about Paul, a boy who had a very successful but stern dad. Dad was busy and never really had time to bond with Paul, yet Paul was expected to follow in his grand footsteps. He would have been a child at lack of a father's love, and that type of male will want to hook up with a female as quickly as possible to fill the void. He also will not want to take nurturing time on her. As he has not been nurtured himself, he will have nothing to offer in that department. So, he will choose a woman quickly, and she will have to be a looker. I suppose that may be what he did, but he chose the wrong woman and got badly burned. An angry hard done by woman. Kicked to the curb in the name of a loving God who she personally cannot feel love from and additionally, she may still have believed that Jesus was a threat to pious Israel as Paul previously did. As they say, 'hell hath no fury like a woman scorned'... A hurt feminine energy can be a volatile one. This, I think, is the evidence of it. 2 Corinthians 12:7;
"And lest I should be exalted above measure through the abundance of the revelations, there was given to me a thorn in the flesh, the messenger of Satan to buffet me, lest I should be exalted above measure."
'Trouble' in the flesh is a partner, 1 Corinthians 7:28-29;

"But and if thou marry, thou hast not sinned; and if a virgin marry, she hath not sinned. Nevertheless such shall have trouble in the flesh: but I spare you. But this I say, brethren, the time is short: it remaineth, that both they that have wives be as though they had none;…"

A thorn is a euphemism for an irritating person, Numbers 33:55, Judges 2:3, Joshua 23:13;

"But if ye will not drive out the inhabitants of the land from before you; then it shall come to pass, that those which ye let remain of them shall be pricks in your eyes, and thorns in your sides, and shall vex you in the land wherein ye dwell."

"Wherefore I also said, I will not drive them out from before you; but they shall be as thorns in your sides, and their gods shall be a snare unto you."

Note the use of 'thorn' with 'side', reflecting the way God created woman from the side of man.

"Know for a certainty that the Lord your God will no more drive out any of these nations from before you; but they shall be snares and traps unto you, and scourges in your sides, and thorns in your eyes, until ye perish from off this good land which the Lord your God hath given you."

As we know, Peter did not always leave a person's side for honourable reasons (Luke 22:57, John 18:17, Mark 14:71, Matthew 26:74).

It was a common theme among early disciples to leave their wives and families, Mark 10:28,29;

"Then Peter began to say unto him, Lo, we have left all, and have followed thee. And Jesus answered and said, Verily I say unto you, There is no man that hath left house, or brethren, or sisters, or father, or mother, or wife, or children, or lands, for my sake, and the gospel's,.."

But you are not going to up and leave without consent from your wife, leaving your own family destitute, ('Physician, heal thyself', 'By their fruits you will know them') unless you have put such maintenance in order as that given by Paul. Now, if God was not in your Join from the get go and you knowingly attached yourself to the wrong woman in error, then a thorn in the flesh is probably going to be the size of it.

Okay, we can see Paul's opinion that it is good not to be Joined, differs from both Proverbs18:22 and Malachi 2&4.

1 Corinthians 7:32-40 abridged;

"But I would have you without carefulness. He that is unmarried careth for the things that belong to the Lord, how he may please the Lord: But he that is married careth for the things that are of the world, how he may please his wife. There is difference also between a wife and a virgin. The unmarried woman careth for the things of the Lord, that she may be holy both in body and in spirit … But she is happier if she so abide, after my judgment: and I think also that I have the Spirit of God."

The rest of what Paul says above on the issue of to be or not to be Joined, I hope through what has been outlined, you can use your own wisdom to arbitrate. Apart from the fact that he is differing vastly from God Himself in Proverbs 18:22, and such in your face issues as earnestly looking for the right partner (Ruth and Boaz, Jacob and Rebecca etc), to ultimately produce Jesus/make a way for Israel; I think that the man is talking from a hurting place.

Ladies, you know what that looks like on a man. Like I say, read the bible like as if the thing is actually real. You will get a lot more out of it and begin to love and care for the characters.

So keep that in mind always when you see what Paul has to say about women. Know that he is not talking from malice, he is just guarding a safe place of peace regarding women through his own spirit.

As a member of the Body of Christ you need to protect your spirit. If you happen to be Joined to someone who does not believe, whether they have never believed or whether even worse they have stopped believing, you only stay with them as long as they are pleased to be with you. I.e. they don't give you grief when you are doing the things of God. And as Paul says, you may be the one to turn them to Jesus or back to Jesus.

Paul says that he speaks on the rest of Join issues not as a commandment from the Lord. Therefore we can glean that there may be more permutations of situations in this rest for Join templates. If so, I believe we should use common disciples-of-Christ sense to determine what should be done in each circumstance, whilst remembering that God in the new contract will speak Himself to all of His children, 1 John 2:27;

"But the anointing which ye have received of him abideth in you, and ye need not that any man teach you: but as the same anointing teacheth you of all things, and is truth, and is no lie, and even as it hath taught you, ye shall abide in him."

Remember, this is John writing to Israel; not having been called to preach to the gentiles who knew little to nothing about the God of Abraham, Isaac and Jacob. Gentiles may be in need of a teacher, at least in the first instance.

Paul speaks on behalf of God for those gentile couples for whom it is possible to 'change mutually' for the better towards God. In 1 Corinthians 7:12 he speaks as a man and not of commandment to unbelievers married to believers. As mentioned earlier, this can also include a spouse who is operating as an unbeliever, having once believed. It is still the same; darkness and light. How can we discern this of a spouse? First of all the bible tells us that if one is to turn their back on the Lord after hearing His word it is a terrible thing for them. They are in a desperate and worse situation spiritually than an unbeliever and only the Lord can bring them out. And even in that, He is not pleased. Hebrews 10:38,39;

"Now the just shall live by faith: but if draw back[5288]**,** (5288, 'hypostello', to withhold under, out of sight, to cover, shrink, conceal, shun, withdraw) **my soul shall have no pleasure in him. But we are not of them who draw back unto perdition; but of them that believe to the saving of the soul."**

However, It is no use thinking you can stay and pull them out of hell if they; either as a believer drawn back or an unbeliever, have chosen not to live with you and be 'pleased to dwell with you'.

How can you tell? This is where 1 John 2:27 comes in handy. Well it is not astrophysics. Hear from God and take note of the things that are happening around you. One of which could be when people prophesy over you as a family or as a couple for good or when you agree as a family to move forward for the good, and your spouse just keeps negating and reneging on God – then the worst has begun to happen in their life. When the will of God is never enough for them.

Chapter 1

Part 2   Prophesy

Malachi tells us that God was no longer accepting the tears of men at the altar because husbands were dealing treacherously with the wives of their youth. Malachi is the final book from the prophets of the Old Covenant so we do well to pay attention. God says she is his companion and a wife of his (the husband's) covenant. The Lord has made the two one in Joining. In Revelation 19:10 John says;

"And I fell at his feet to worship him. And he said unto me, See thou do it not: I am thy fellow servant, and of thy brethren that have the testimony of Jesus: worship God: for the testimony of Jesus is the spirit of prophecy."

As he sees the things that are to happen and becomes overwhelmed, the angel tells John not to worship him. The angel says, that by the simple giving of a testimony with evidence of Jesus in our lives, we can predict the future. 2 Peter 1:21 says;

"For the prophecy came not in old time by the will of man[444]: but holy men[444] of God spake moved by the Holy Ghost."

444 here is 'anthropos' and means 'mankind', 'people'. We know that many women in the bible were great prophets and teachers. To name a few: Deborah, Huldah, Noadiah, Anna, Philip's four daughters, Rachel, Hannah, Abigail, Elisabeth, and Mary.

Let us know this first before we go on, 2 Peter 1:20;

"...that no prophecy of the scripture is of any private interpretation."

Now, God himself tells us that He fully expects women to prophesy, Acts 2:17,18, 21:9;

"And it shall come to pass in the last days, saith God, I will pour out of my Spirit upon all flesh: and your sons and your daughters shall prophesy, and your young men shall see visions, and your old men shall dream dreams: And on my servants and on my handmaidens I will pour out in those days of my Spirit; and they shall prophesy:.."

"And the same man had four daughters, virgins, which did prophesy."

In view of the fact that following a prophecy from one of any of these gals, God's hand moves, I would suggest you let them speak. Note the bible's placement of the colon. Information following a colon is the result of information preceding it.

"...my handmaidens I will pour out in those days of my Spirit; and they shall prophesy: And I will shew wonders in heaven above, and signs in the earth beneath; blood, and fire, and vapour of smoke: ..."

Don't mess with the handmaidens of God in these last days. You are likely to get burned.

Paul says in 1 Timothy 2:11-15;

"Let the woman learn in silence[2271] with all subjection[5292]. But I suffer[2010] not a woman to teach[1321], nor to usurp[8321] authority over the man, but to be in silence[2271]. For Adam was first formed, then Eve[2096]. And Adam was not deceived[538], but the woman[1135] being deceived was in the transgression[3847]. Notwithstanding she shall be saved[4982] in childbearing[5042], if they[3306] continue in faith and charity and holiness with sobriety[4997]."

Paul, is a misunderstood man. Men think he is stroking their ego, and women think he is annihilating them. Paul is doing neither. Let us look at what he is actually saying by translating the Greek into English properly using the Strong's numbers.

"Let the woman[1135] learn in hésuchia[2271]calmness (this does not mean speechlessness, that word is sigé[4602]) with all hupotagé[5292]control of herself. But epitrepó[2010]personally, I trust not a woman to didaskó[1321]teach continuously, nor to authenteó[8321]try to authenticate herself as a male, but to be in hésuchia[2271]calmness. For man was first formed, then Heua[2096]the good, And man was not apataó[538]led into error, but guné[1135]the generated one exapataó[1818]one and all, parabasis[3847]overstepped. Notwithstanding ginomai[1096]+sózó[4982]healing will emerge in teknogonia[5042]the equipment of a womb, if menó[3306]she stays continually in faith and charity and holiness with sóphrosuné[4997]good use of her mind."

Wow. Now to me that looks completely different. Paul says that a woman should be calm.

The rest, he says, is just his opinion.

However, that opinion is good. Paul is a good loving man. He is all the while thinking about protecting the calmness and elegance of womanhood. Have you noticed that all the modern day male evangelists just keep preaching year in year out without a break, 24/7 it seems? On and on, telling us different renderings of the same snippets of the bible. By the way, that whole celebrity/preacher/mega-church issue finished in 1998 when God, through a mega church, crushed the attempt of the devil to take over all of West Africa.

Anyway, I wouldn't want to be continually preaching or teaching when I was on a heavy period. Would you? I don't want to be a bloke. Ladies, do you?

Paul purposefully switches to the use of 'Adam' with the word 'Eve'. Then he switches back to 'Adam' with the word 'woman'. What does that mean? It means that he is protecting the gentle delicately bespoke nature and purpose of woman when created as 'Eve'. He is simply saying that we need to add a touch of class to ourselves and realise there is something special about us women that opens doors and can create new realities, Genesis 3:20;

"And Adam called his wife's name Eve[2332]; ('chwvh' Chet, Wav, Hey; The separation has secured the revelation) **because she was the mother of all living."**

Adam, bless him, he did well; little honey. This special gifting is in the yet untold function of our wombs; whether we have had, or can have children, or not, it is in the equipment. With full knowledge of the mystery of this glory you and that womb of yours can physically move you and hubby off of this planet into others; a precept the same as bringing a baby spirit and body here from heaven through the womb, going in the other trajectory (Matthew 18:10).

If you think about it, it's like when God said to the Babylonians that if they kept up, they would become like Him in Genesis 11:6;

"And the Lord said, Behold, the people is one, and they have all one language; and this they begin to do: and now nothing will be restrained from them, which they have imagined to do."

Think on it. He didn't say that the Babylonians did anything wrong, just that they were about to break loose and become omnipresent, omniscient and omnipotent like Him.

Now parallel that with what He said to Eve and Adam in Genesis 3:22, 23;

"And the Lord God said, Behold, the man is become as one of us, to know good and evil: and now, lest he put forth his hand, and take also of the tree of life, and eat, and live for ever: Therefore the Lord God sent him forth from the garden of Eden, to till the ground from whence he was taken."

The fall in the garden of Eden was due to a bit of misplaced forward thinking from Eve, that was it; she overstepped and didn't do her homework. She should have asked God directly what the four-one-nine was. She got her information second hand from Adam who himself was told by God what he needed to hear. That sufficed his understanding. However Eve was a different kind of creation being double formed from Adam's side. The result was a creation more internally spiritually keen. Had she been more aware of who she was she would have gone direct to God to ask for what she needed to know regarding the tree, that was her problem. We shall go into that later.

Paul is just asking for women to do him a favour and chill, act classy and think with God before they speak as a god. Psalm 82:6;
"I have said, Ye are gods; and all of you are children of the most High."

In fact Eve did not get any curses on exit from Eden. Adam did.

For some reason these 'experts' have translated the words denoting the female in Genesis all wrong. I wonder why.
Okay let's break it all down.

Genesis 1:26, she is called 'man' by God;
"And God said, Let us make man[120] in our image,.."
120 is 'adm' Aleph, Dalet, Mem; The first strong door into life.

Genesis 1:27, she is called 'female' by Moses;
"...male and female[5347] created he them."
5347 is 'wvnqbh' Wav, Noon, Qoof, Bet, Hey; The hook of life is revealed last from inside'.

Genesis 1:28, she and he are called 'them' by Moses;
"And God blessed them[853]..."

853 is 'atm' Aleph, Tav, Mem (atom); The first sign of life.

Genesis 1:28, she and he are called 'them' again by Moses;
"...and God said unto them?..."
There is no number in my dictionary for this Hebrew word 'lhm' Lamed, Hey, Mem; The controller reveals life.

Genesis 1:29, she and he are called 'you' by God;
"I have given you⁸⁵³..."
853 ' 'ach' Aleph, Chet; The first separation.

Genesis 1:29, she and he are called 'them' by God;
"...to you it shall be for meat."
There is no number in my dictionary for this Hebrew word 'lkm' Lamed, Kaf, Mem; The controller allows life.

Genesis 2:18, she is called 'a helper' by God;
"...I will make him an help⁵⁸²⁸ meet for him."
5828 'uzr' masculine noun, Ayin, Zayin, Reysh; To see the cut person.

Genesis 2:23, she is called 'she' and 'woman' by Adam;
"...she²⁰⁶³ shall be called Woman⁸⁰², because she²⁰⁶³ was taken out of Man³⁷⁶..."
2063, 'zat' in the Hebrew language is 'likewise'. 802 is 'ashh', Aleph, Sheen, Hey; The first strong destroyer is revealed. (Incidentally, 'man' here is 'ash', 376; Aleph, Sheen; The first destroyer.)

Genesis 2:24, she is called 'wife' by Adam;
"...and shall cleave unto his wife⁸⁰²?..."
802 'ashchwv', Aleph, Sheen, Chet, Wav; The strong devourer separates additions.

Genesis 3:20, she is called 'mother' by Adam;
"...because she was the mother⁵¹⁷ of all living."
517 'em', Aleph, Mem; Strong life.

The marvellous handiwork of God.
Adam prophetically called her 'ashh', in Genesis 2:23. The words God later spoke to the serpent in Genesis 3:15 were;

"And I will put enmity between thee and the woman[802], and between thy seed and her seed; it shall bruise thy head, and thou shalt bruise his heel."

Note that in the above scripture God also calls her 'ashh'; The first strong destroyer is revealed.

So, not to cut a long story short, our Paul is just trying to protect all this luverliness in women. So don't hate on him ladies, and gentlemen don't recoil at the low status of women as a result of what you thought Paul was saying.

Our Paul on how to conduct oneself in a gathering, 1 Corinthians 14:31-40;

"For ye may all prophesy one by one, that all may learn, and all may be comforted. And the spirits of the prophets are subject to the prophets. For God is not the author of confusion, but of peace[1515], as in all churches of the saints.

Let your women keep silence in the churches: for it is not permitted unto them to speak; but they are commanded to be under obedience as also saith the law. And if they will learn any thing, let them ask their husbands at home: for it is a shame for women to speak in the church.

What? came the word of God out from you? or came it unto you only?

If any man think himself to be a prophet, or spiritual, let him acknowledge that the things that I write unto you are the commandments of the Lord. But if any man be ignorant, let him be ignorant. Wherefore, brethren, covet to prophesy, and forbid not to speak with tongues. Let all things be done decently and in order."

Let me take the liberty of repeating that again, so as to make sure ya'll read it;

"What? came the word of God out from you? or came it unto you only?"

A five-year-old could read that and understand.

Paul is saying DO NOT TELL WOMEN THEY MUST KEEP SILENCE ASKING THEIR HUSBANDS QUESTIONS WHEN THEY GET HOME. IT IS NOT A SHAME FOR THEM TO SPEAK.

The Corinthians were obviously overtaken with a group of macho men, 'experts' that they were. Paul tells them bluntly; What are you on about? Did you write the word of God? Was the word of God written for you daft men only and not for your women? Sounds like the daft males who began the roman catholic church.

I like Paul. He pulls no punches and takes no prisoners. 1515 is the Greek Strong's number for peace, 'eirene'; to set at one again, to join together as a whole, 'properly, wholeness, i.e. when all essential parts are joined together; peace (God's gift of wholeness).' This is the ultimate plan of God. To create men and women who are fearless *together* in the face of all adversity that this planet has to obstruct us. And then we can move on to other planets and other things.

Now to the mislead men (and women) out there regarding the reading of scripture. Can you read? Then always give the whole chapter in context, and so let the people taste and see that the Lord IS good. Don't give the people a mouthful of pepper and tell them it's dinner. Deliver the whole meal; all of the ingredients.

So ladies don't be scared, God actually and really wants only good for you and has set a bountiful table of wonder before us that we need to get together and start to enjoy. Ephesians 5:20-23;

"Giving thanks always for all things unto God and the Father in the name of our Lord Jesus Christ; Submitting yourselves[5293] one to another in the fear of God. Wives, submit yourselves unto your own husbands, as unto the Lord."

5293 is hypotásso a combination of the words hypo (5295) meaning 'under' and tásso (5021) meaning 'arrange' – properly, 'under God's arrangement,' i.e. submitting to the Lord (His plan). Like arranging yourself under your husband, to catch the blessings being thrown from God, through hubby, to you. Men can make prosperity like magic, no work or toil involved. When they Join onto you and get out from under their curse given in Genesis God automatically blesses them (Proverbs 18:22).

You ladies are not some lowly creation under men in general, you line up behind your own husbands so that angels can minister to the family unit in order. Submission has nothing to do with staying at home, the kitchen or the washing up. Roles are something you as a couple decide upon based on what you decide on. God does not care who does the washing up.

'As unto the Lord' signifies the spirit in which Sarah submitted to Abraham and called him 'lord' (1 Peter 3:6, Genesis 18:12). When she called Abraham 'lord' in Genesis she was talking in her mind. She didn't even say it out loud. Now to me, that is stronger and more meaningful because she really felt and knew the full love and protection that Abraham had in his great relationship with God and his great respect for her as a strong, opinionated wise woman from the Creator. Incidentally, they were both born from the same father; being half brother and sister. That is one reason why they knew and trusted each other so much, because they grew up together in their father's house. We as Joined couples are supposed to be growing up together in our Father's house just like these two. It is then that nations are born and miracles may begin to happen. She called Abraham 'my lord' Genesis 18:12;

"Therefore Sarah laughed within herself, saying, After I am waxed old shall I have pleasure, my lord[113] being old also?"

113 is wvadnh, Wav, Aleph, Dalet, Noon, Hey; The security of the first door into life is revealed. Literally meaning the security Abraham affords her from God. So, no problem there then.

Okay, so this is the order: Ephesians 5:23,24;

"For the husband is the head of the wife, even as Christ is the head of the church: and he is the saviour of the body. Therefore as the church is subject unto Christ, so let the wives be to their own husbands in every thing."

Yeah, and like I said above, this is the great mystery verse 27-31;

"That he might present it to himself a glorious church, not having spot, or wrinkle, or any such thing; but that it should be holy and without blemish. So ought men to love their wives as their own bodies. He that loveth his wife loveth himself. For no man ever yet hated his own flesh; but nourisheth and cherisheth it, even as the Lord the church: For we are members of his body, of his flesh, and of his bones. For this cause shall a man leave his father and mother, and shall be joined unto his wife, and they two shall be one flesh."

The thing all sits in the husband and wife. Particularly we need the husband to prepare his wife as if he individually is preparing that wife to marry Jesus. Like perfecting her inwardly and outwardly.

Now, respect where respect is due to the wife 1 Peter 3:1-7;

"Likewise, ye wives, be in subjection to your own husbands; that, if any obey not the word, they also may without the word be won by the conversation of the wives; While they behold your chaste conversation coupled with fear. Whose adorning let it not be that outward adorning of plaiting the hair, and of wearing of gold, or of putting on of apparel; But let it be the hidden man of the heart, in that which is not corruptible, even the ornament of a meek and quiet spirit, which is in the sight of God of great price. For after this manner in the old time the holy women also, who trusted in God, adorned themselves, being in subjection unto their own husbands: Even as Sara obeyed Abraham, calling him lord: whose daughters ye are, as long as ye do well, and are not afraid with any amazement. Likewise, ye husbands, dwell with them according to knowledge, giving honour unto the wife, as unto the weaker vessel, and as being heirs together of the grace of life; that your prayers be not hindered."

The original Greek reads thusly, verse 7;

"Husbands likewise, dwelling with according to knowledge, as with a weaker vessel with the female, rendering honour, as also joint-heirs of grace of life, so as for not to be hindered the prayers of you."

I mean, thusly.., I actually think that Paul is saying the man is the weaker vessel. Adam falsely accused Eve in the garden, if he was right, then he would have stopped her. The snake hadn't accused anybody of anything yet. The word 'false accuser' is 1228 in Strong's Greek = diabolos, which means 'devil' (in the Old Testament, there is no such word as 'devil'. It is a false translation of the worship of goats and bull-colossus'). This leads me to believe that it took until the new contract when men had got so detached from their wives and the pure purposes of God, that satan and his cohort were really able to speak against, and manifest in people as devils). Anyway, I digress. God so kind, He did not call Adam a devil. But Eve was not cursed, she was held back by God as a result of her wrongdoings. Adam was the one who got the curse because of his wrongdoings meaning his vessel is weaker, Genesis 3:16-19;

"Unto the woman he said, I will greatly multiply thy sorrow and thy conception; in sorrow thou shalt bring forth children; and thy desire shall be to thy husband, and he shall rule over thee. And unto Adam he said, Because thou hast hearkened unto the voice of thy wife, and hast eaten of the tree, of which I commanded thee, saying, Thou shalt not eat of it: cursed is the ground for thy sake;

in sorrow shalt thou eat of it all the days of thy life; Thorns also and thistles shall it bring forth to thee; and thou shalt eat the herb of the field; In the sweat of thy face shalt thou eat bread, till thou return unto the ground; for out of it wast thou taken: for dust thou art, and unto dust shalt thou return."

Eve wasn't taken out of the earth, she was taken from Adam's side.
The mandate for our men now is Romans 12:21;
"Be not overcome of evil[2556]**(worthlessness), but overcome evil with good**[18]**(benefit).**

Some of us want to see Jesus and live with Him and be glad. So can we move this thing along please? Can the crusty crispyones stop the nonsense and tell the Body of Christ what is really in these scriptures or move graciously to one side while we search them ourselves. This is important information.

Genesis 20:3
"But God came to Abimelech in a dream by night, and said to him, Behold, thou art but a dead man, for the woman which thou hast taken; for she is a man's wife."
That is not what the original scripture says at all. Translated more appropriately Genesis 20:3 says;
"But came God to Abimelech in a dream by night, and said to him, Behold, you a dead man, for the woman which you have taken – the same[1931]**wvhwva**   **is a master who guards**[1166]**bulch** (Bet, Ayin, Lamed, Chet; Inside seeing the controller, fences)   **a master**[1167]**bul** (Bet, Ayin, Lamed; Inside seeing the controller)**."**

Stunning.

"So Abraham prayed unto God: and God healed Abimelech, and his wife, and his maidservants; and they bare children. For the Lord had fast closed up all the wombs of the house of Abimelech, because of Sarah Abraham's wife."

She must have been there a while. Anyway, Sarah was master guardian and stalwart fence around all of master Abraham's proceedings. Wow.

What are these preacher guys telling us? What back water have they studied the bible in? In fact, what bibles are they studying in their seminaries/cemeteries? It is certainly not the one from God.

Because of Sarah's presence in the house, being there because Abraham was scared of Abimalech, God shut the whole house down. I don't know what Abraham was thinking, but Abimalech had the good God given sense not to sleep with Sarah. Sarah was probably full of prayer all the while she was there, knowing that she loved Abraham. He was scared, but she trusted God to throw her full blessing through Abraham by submitting to Abraham's decision. So, she got it. In fact, they both did. Abraham came out of that situation with;

"And Abimelech took sheep, and oxen, and menservants, and womenservants, and gave them unto Abraham, and restored him Sarah his wife. And Abimelech said, Behold, my land is before thee: dwell where it pleaseth thee. And unto Sarah he said, Behold, I have given thy brother a thousand pieces of silver: behold, he is to thee a covering of the eyes, unto all that are with thee, and with all other: ~~thus she was reproved~~. So Abraham prayed unto God: and God healed Abimelech, and his wife, and his maidservants; and they bare children."

It does not say 'thus she was reproved'. It says; Wav, Noon, Kaf, Chet, Tav; The security of life allows the fencing of the sign. That looks to me like Abimalech was saying God was keeping Sarah's womb clear for Abraham's seed, so that from Abraham's loins Jesus could come without Sarah being defiled. God bless Abimalech. He too was a righteous man. He told Sarah (then Sarai) that Abraham (then Abram) was 'a covering of the eyes'. This meant that she and Abraham should no longer be worried about another man snatching her away from Abraham and causing harm or violence to Abraham as a result of her good looks.

Women, we need to wake up and now. It is time we knew who we are. Fellas, it is time to make a move. Only a crazy woman would look at what God has given us, and want something else.

Revelation 2:20;
"Notwithstanding I have a few things against thee, because thou sufferest that woman Jezebel, which calleth herself a prophetess, to teach and to seduce my servants to commit fornication, and to eat things sacrificed unto idols."

Mark 6:14-29;

And king Herod heard of him; (for his name was spread abroad:) and he said, That John the Baptist was risen from the dead, and therefore mighty works do shew forth themselves in him...Herod himself had sent forth and laid hold upon John, and bound him in prison for Herodias' sake, his brother Philip's wife: for he had married her. For John had said unto Herod, It is not lawful for thee to have thy brother's wife. Therefore Herodias had a quarrel against him, and would have killed him; but she could not: For Herod feared John, knowing that he was a just man and an holy, and observed him; and when he heard him, he did many things, and heard him gladly...And when the daughter of the said Herodias came in, and danced, and pleased Herod and them that sat with him, the king said unto the damsel, Ask of me whatsoever thou wilt, and I will give it thee. And he sware unto her, Whatsoever thou shalt ask of me, I will give it thee, unto the half of my kingdom. And she went forth, and said unto her mother, What shall I ask? And she said, The head of John the Baptist. And she came in straightway with haste unto the king, and asked, saying, I will that thou give me by and by in a charger the head of John the Baptist. And the king was exceeding sorry; yet for his oath's sake, and for their sakes which sat with him, he would not reject her. And immediately the king sent an executioner, and commanded his head to be brought: and he went and beheaded him in the prison, And brought his head in a charger, and gave it to the damsel: and the damsel gave it to her mother. And when his disciples heard of it, they came and took up his corpse, and laid it in a tomb."

1 Kings 19: 1-3;

"And Ahab told Jezebel all that Elijah had done, and withal how he had slain all the prophets with the sword. Then Jezebel sent a messenger unto Elijah, saying, So let the gods do to me, and more also, if I make not thy life as the life of one of them by to morrow about this time. And when he saw that, he arose, and went for his life, and came to Beersheba, which belongeth to Judah, and left his servant there."

Jezebel is a female that pops up when average men need a leader and good men are tired. Elijah was tired when he encountered this female and King Ahab did not know his left from his right.

This, ladies and gentlemen, is our main adversary. We need to gang up against her. We need to just ignore everything about her, stop giving her room in our gatherings to expound her rubbish about agreeing with the crap position we women should have of being less than men. She pretends she has taken wise counsel, whilst stroking men's egos in some fiendish insatiable and unsatiable cause. If you notice, she always disrespects her sisters around her, isolates them, and tries to authenticate herself as a man; just as Paul warned against in 1 Timothy 2:12. She speaks as a daft man and fully embraces the idea that *other* women should shut up and submit. And there she is, talking nonsense until the cows come home and daft men cannot see the wood for the tresses.

To all you daft Jezebels; nobody cares about you.

To all you daft men, wake up and repent; you are being had.

And to those men who already know God has given women such liberty through His scriptures, yet are still perpetuating the lie; God says that you are perpetrating a fraud on Him, you've been caught and He will deal with you accordingly.

Chapter 1

Part 3   Take Cover

And now that word used by Paul, dreaded by all women; 'submit'.
Sisters, let me clean it up for you. Ephesians 5:21-31;
**"Submitting yourselves one to another in the fear of God. Wives,
~~submit yourselves~~ unto your own husbands, as unto the Lord. For
the husband is the head of the wife, even as Christ is the head of
the church: and he is the saviour of the body. Therefore as the
church is subject unto Christ, so let the wives be to their own
husbands in every thing. Husbands, love your wives, even as
Christ also loved the church, and gave himself for it; That he might
sanctify and cleanse it with the washing of water by the word, That
he might present it to himself a glorious church, not having spot,
or wrinkle, or any such thing; but that it should be holy and
without blemish. So ought men to love their wives as their own
bodies. He that loveth his wife loveth himself. For no man ever yet
hated his own flesh; but nourisheth and cherisheth it, even as the
Lord the church: For we are members of his body, of his flesh, and
of his bones. For this cause shall a man leave his father and
mother, and shall be joined unto his wife, and they two shall be
one flesh."**
Do you know that just to help us ladies out, Paul never wrote 'submit' in
verse 22. Those crispy crusty Crispyones put it in here by their own evil
choice just to make you feel bad. It is not there. Check the original
Greek text. He just said something like 'each wife, look to your own
husband'.
**"Wives, to the own husbands, as to the Lord, for husband is head
of the wife,.."**

If you look at the previous discourse he was having with the Greek
congregation in Ephesus you will see that there had probably been some
incident where a married woman innocently had a prayer meeting or
something with a man that wasn't her husband. As a result there were
probably rumours and gossip flying around and she also possibly
harmlessly took this man's counsel on something.
Harmless as it may have seemed, had she only obtained her husband's
permission to go to see this brother in the first place, all negative energy

35

concerning the innocent liaison would have been diverted by the angels (as we saw with Sarah in Abimalech's house). That is what submit means. It's a covering. It means it doesn't rain bad on you.

Here Paul ends with the beginning of the unfurling of what this Great mystery is between the man and his wife. I bet he knows what it is now; but he didn't then. The mystery begins with the fact that as each man treats his wife like a queen, nourishing her, only her, cherishing her, purchasing the finest clothes for her (as Solomon was arrayed), loving her, giving his life for her; she evolves into another creation of God, entire. It is she that then spiritually begins to usher in the glory of God, nourished by her man, of equivalent mass to the potency needed for the end times.
And that's it ladies. I now pronounce you man and free she.

So, we need to be able to properly read what God is saying in our bibles, by viewing the original Hebrew and Greek texts.

Was the new testament really written in Greek? It is hard to study the text fully as I have no connection with the linguistics. Greece? Great, but what does Greece represent spiritually regarding faith? Not a whole lot.
The Greeks were famous for founding the belief that the womb in a woman roamed throughout her body. It was this roaming, according to them which gave rise to her mood swings and inability to control her emotions. As a result, they named the womb 'hysteria'. So, their women had hysterias, were hysterical, and when it all got too much for their men they were given hysterectomies.
Ignorance gone to sea.
In addition, the 'New Testament' does not become the new covenant until the book of Acts, after the shedding of blood which pre-empts the brokering of every real contract. The books from Matthew, Mark, Luke and John are part of the Old Testament so why do we have to read it in Greek?
Suffice to say that I have no affinity with the Greek text of the new contract. I wish I had it in Hebrew. Some of the Greek words given in translation of the text just do not seem to fit. Unlike the Old Testament, I cannot isolate each letter and see what God was really saying. However, I am aware that God is not powerless. And so therefore, when I read the new contract, although it is the most important for me as a woman of God, I take the words on the face value given. I am sure that clever God can pick up the slack.

Paul says that he was called to the gentiles, Ephesians 3:1-6

"For this cause I Paul, the prisoner of Jesus Christ for you Gentiles, If ye have heard of the dispensation of the grace of God which is given me to you-ward: How that by revelation he made known unto me the mystery;… as it is now revealed unto his holy apostles and prophets by the Spirit; That the Gentiles should be fellowheirs, and of the same body, and partakers of his promise in Christ by the gospel:.."

and in Romans 1:16;

"For I am not ashamed of the gospel of Christ: for it is the power of God unto salvation to every one that believeth; to the Jew first, and also to the Greek."

Ephesians 4:17;

"This I say therefore, and testify in the Lord, that ye henceforth walk not as other Gentiles walk,…"

By contrast, Jesus was not, Mark 7:26-28;

"The woman was a Greek, a Syrophenician by nation; and she besought him that he would cast forth the devil out of her daughter. But Jesus said unto her, 'Let the children first be filled: for it is not meet to take the children's bread, and to cast it unto the dogs'. And she answered and said unto him, Yes, Lord: yet the dogs under the table eat of the children's crumbs."

and Matthew 15:22-28

"And, behold, a woman of Canaan came out of the same coasts, and cried unto him, saying, Have mercy on me, O Lord, thou son of David; my daughter is grievously vexed with a devil. But he answered her not a word. And his disciples came and besought him, saying, Send her away; for she crieth after us. But he answered and said, 'I am not sent but unto the lost sheep of the house of Israel'. Then came she and worshipped him, saying, Lord, help me. But he answered and said, 'It is not meet to take the children's bread, and to cast it to dogs'. And she said, Truth, Lord: yet the dogs eat of the crumbs which fall from their masters' table. Then Jesus answered and said unto her, 'O woman, great is thy faith: be it unto thee even as thou wilt'. And her daughter was made whole from that very hour."

Now, how was it possible for the disciples to tell just from looking at her that she was not an Israelite? In Matthew 8 and Luke 7 the Greek/gentile centurion sent Jewish elders to ask Jesus for help;

"And when Jesus was entered into Capernaum, there came[4334] unto him a centurion, beseeching him, And saying, Lord, my servant lieth at home sick of the palsy, grievously tormented. And Jesus saith unto him, 'I will come and heal him'. The centurion answered and said, Lord, I am not worthy that thou shouldest come under my roof: but speak the word only, and my servant shall be healed. For I am a man under authority, having soldiers under me: and I say to this man, Go, and he goeth; and to another, Come, and he cometh; and to my servant, Do this, and he doeth it. When Jesus heard it, he marvelled, and said to them that followed, 'Verily I say unto you, I have not found so great faith, no, not in Israel. And I say unto you, That many shall come from the east and west, and shall sit down with Abraham, and Isaac, and Jacob, in the kingdom of heaven. But the children of the kingdom shall be cast out into outer darkness: there shall be weeping and gnashing of teeth'. And Jesus said unto the centurion, 'Go thy way; and as thou hast believed, so be it done unto thee'. And his servant was healed in the selfsame hour."

In Strong's 4334 'came' is defined as 'I come near, consent to'. However the pure sense of one's physical arrival is given in Matthew 2:1 where 3854 'arrived' is defined as 'I appear, come, arrive at'. Now review the second account of the request from the centurion.

"And when he heard of Jesus, he sent unto him the elders of the Jews, beseeching him that he would come and heal his servant. And when they came[3854] to Jesus, they besought him instantly, saying, That he was worthy for whom he should do this: For he loveth our nation, and he hath built us a synagogue. Then Jesus went with them. And when he was now not far from the house, the centurion sent friends to him, saying unto him, Lord, trouble not thyself: for I am not worthy that thou shouldest enter under my roof: Wherefore neither thought I myself worthy to come unto thee: but say in a word, and my servant shall be healed. For I also am a man set under authority, having under me soldiers, and I say unto one, Go, and he goeth; and to another, Come, and he cometh; and to my servant, Do this, and he doeth it. When Jesus heard these things, he marvelled at him, and turned him about, and said unto the people that followed him, 'I say unto you, I have not found so great faith, no, not in Israel'."

Jesus was sent to the twelve clans of Israel and He noted only two times in the bible 'great faith'. He attributed this great faith to two gentiles. He went on to state that these would also take full part in the inheritance of God, but some natural born children of God caught up in the lies of this world, would not. Paul was a natural born Israelite of the clan Benjamin, ministering to Greeks. As we have seen above, the disciples could tell the Greek woman was not an Israelite by her appearance only. Jesus' hair is like wool, and His body is the colour of fine brass burned/polished bronze. Paul says in 1 Timothy 2:5-10;

"For there is one God, and one mediator between God and men, the man Christ Jesus; Who gave himself a ransom for all, to be testified in due time. Whereunto I am ordained a preacher, and an apostle, (I speak the truth in Christ, and lie not;) a teacher of the Gentiles in faith and verity. I will therefore that men pray every where, lifting up holy hands, without wrath and doubting. In like manner also, that women adorn themselves in modest apparel, with shamefacedness and sobriety; not with broided hair, or gold, or pearls, or costly array; But (which becometh women professing godliness) with good works."

As a woman possessing hair that is like wool, and a body the colour of fine burnished brass, I can testify that unless I am sporting a short fro, if my hair is not in plaits then I have not finished getting ready to leave my house. A longer afro requires that you plait it or else, you will loose it. These Greek women did not have afros but were attempting in good faith to emulate the hairstyles of an afro wearing woman. When a Caucasian/Aryan woman plaits her hair, it is not the same as that of an African woman's plaited hair.

Afro hair is an automated substance which does not leave the scalp as a dead entity. It contains a high amount of active melanin and the tighter the coil pattern the more potent its activation of certain spiritual precedence. Nazarenes took vows in the bible to signify in the spirit that they were 'locked in' to one ministry on the earth. Samson and Jesus' cousin John were two such men. The Nazerite vow required a specific diet and no cutting of the hair, Samson had seven locks; Judges 16:13.

In 1 Timothy 2, Paul was talking to Greek people without afro hair, and is therefore addressing the fact that this straighter braided hair, probably flicked to and fro during gatherings, was beginning to become a distraction and starting a fashion show. If the women all turned up attired like Iris Apfel, I am sure Paul would have entered a tick in the box for elegance and style; problem solved. He also mentions that the men in the congregation were not raising up their hands in demonstration of liberty; being a little subdued. Now, that don't sound like a brother to me. It soundeth very much like a more retiring creed of man who is naturally more reserved.

So, Paul is talking to joint heirs in Christ who do not have afro hair or an African cultural manner.

Paul says to the Corinthians in his first letter 11:3-16;

"... the head of every man is Christ; and the head of the woman is the man; and the head of Christ is God. Every man praying or prophesying, having his head covered[2596]kata(down from), dishonoureth[2617]kataischynei(confuses) his head. But every woman that prayeth or prophesieth with her head uncovered[177]akatakaluptos(unveiled) dishonoureth[2617] her head: for that is even all one as if she were shaven[3587]. For if the woman be not covered, let her also be shorn[2751]: but if it be a shame for a woman to be shorn[2751]keirasthai(cropped, clipped) or shaven[3587] xyrasthai(shave off the hair), let her be covered. For a man indeed ought not to cover his head, forasmuch as he is the image and glory of God: but the woman is the glory of the man. For the man is not of the woman: but the woman of the man. Neither was the man created for the woman; but the woman for the man. For this cause ought the woman to have power on her head because of the angels. Nevertheless neither is the man without the woman, neither the woman without the man, in the Lord. For as the woman is of the man, even so is the man also by the woman; but all things of God. Judge in yourselves: is it comely that a woman pray unto God uncovered? Doth not even nature itself teach you, that, if a man have long hair, it is a shame unto him? But if a woman have long hair, it is a glory to her: for her hair is given her for a covering. But if any man seem to be contentious, we have no such custom, neither the churches of God."

Again this is an example of the differences in hair type between the Israelites and the Greeks. Let me re-iterate, Paul is preaching here to the gentiles. We know that both Samson and John the baptiser had long hair. An African man with long afro hair evokes an entirely different energy than that of a Caucasian man with long hair. When you see an African man with very long hair it can make him look more manly. When you see a Caucasian man with very long hair he seems (and often acts) more effeminately. Similarly, an African woman with a short fro does not look as if she is in danger of burning her bra. However, a Caucasian woman with cropped hair does look more left-of-centre. So Paul is saying that if a Greek man has his hair flowing past his cheeks, the angels may mistake him for a woman. Likewise if a Greek woman has cut her hair too short she may be mistaken for a man.

Paul mentions that Israelites do not have the custom that he is trying to outline to these gentiles, Israelite women having no custom regarding the keeping of their afro hair and Israelite men not being required to keep their hair short. As I said earlier, believe it or don't believe it, afro hair speaks. And so angels can read it and quickly interpret who they are ministering to and how to minister. He then goes on to say that the men in the congregation should not argue with him over that. We know he is not talking about not being contentious in general because he expounds in Galatians 2:11 how he withstood Peter to his face.

In 1 Corinthians 14:34-38 Paul lets, primarily the men, in the Greek/gentile congregation know that he and also God are not ignorant of the fact that they are using Hebrew Old Testament law to justify a display of egotistical male chauvinism toward their women. He tells them plainly, as mentioned earlier, that they are all trippin and should come back to the realities of Love. *What? Were you male Greeks there when the law was delivered to Moses, or has God given a new dispensation of dullness just to you?;*
"Let your women keep silence in the churches: for it is not permitted unto them to speak; but they are commanded to be under obedience as also saith the law. And if they will learn any thing, let them ask their husbands at home: for it is a shame for women to speak in the church. What? came the word of God out from you? or came it unto you only? If any man think himself to be a prophet, or spiritual, let him acknowledge that the things that I write unto you are the commandments of the Lord. But if any man be ignorant, let him be ignorant."
Thank you once again Paul. Throw those chauvinists to the curb.

Sisters, we have our mandate. Let us be free, fellow heirs and fellow partakers in the preaching of the <u>Good</u> News. Not the old donut. It is imperative that we all realise who we are and who the real Hebrews are. Those who do not get this into perspective will soon be caught running out of the anointing and clean out of the presence of God in these last days as we wrap this thing up. Substantiating a God who did not create

Adam and Eve in fully melanated form, and created Jesus as a Caucasian man with straight hair and shaved legs results in non-comprehension of many scriptures. The truth is very clear. Erring from these facts leads to twisting and wickering of one's spirit away from the Truth.

The purposes of God are true, immutable and eternal.

Chapter 2

God's Opinion

Daniel 11:32; "...the people that do know their God[430] shall be strong, and do exploits."

It's good to know God.

The word for God in the above scripture is Strong's number 430 'alhym'. However the word used in the original Hebrew text is actually 'alhywv'. Alhywv consists of the Hebrew letters Aleph, Lamed, Hey, Yood, Wav, and means 'The leading authority reveals what is made and secures it'. We have security in God when we know His character and can predict what He will do next, which gives us the ability to prophesy.

In Genesis 15:2 we are given the word 'Lord' which is Adnh 136 , Aleph, Dalet, Noon, Hey. This is a masculine noun and means 'The leader that opens the door into life is revealed'. Adnh is a form of the word Adwvn 113, Aleph, Dalet, Wav, Noon, also a masculine noun which means 'The leader that opens the door to the security of life'.

Another name we are given for 'God' in the bible is YHWH 3068/3069. YHWH is not directly equal to the word 'God' when translated, it is more like 'Revealer'. The Hebrew letters for YHWH; Yood, Hey, Wav, Hey mean 'The hand that reveals the secure nail of revelation'.

2 Chronicles 28:3 says that
"...the Lord had cast out..."
'Lord' in the original Hebrew script here taken from the Westminster Leningrad Codex is hrysh spelt with the letters Hey, Reysh, Yood, Sheen. Generally this word which appears only once in the Old Testament is translated as just 'Lord' and given the Strong's number 3068 which is for YHWH; Hebrew letters Yood, Hey, Wav, Hey. Different to those in hrysh. Horus is a character in Egyptian history, he was the son of Isis and Osiris. Horus is where we get our word 'Hero'.

YHWH has many characteristics. They are derived from the things that He does; the characteristics that make Him. All these names are prefixed with YHWH in the Strong's. However, in the original Hebrew text they are prefixed by Alhym 430 when we are told what He does, and prefixed by YHWH 3068/3069 when we are told what the benefit of the name is to us. These are the ones that I am aware of:

YHWH yrah 3070 (3068+7200)(yrah) – Yood, Reysh, Aleph, Hey, meaning: The work of the highest leader is revealed = He makes it seen/is my provider. (Incidentally, Reysh, Aleph, Hey, is Rah. Rah is the Sun God in Egyptian history. We will touch on that and the issue of hrysh/Horus in a later chapter.

YHWH nsy 3071 (3068+5251) = my banner, Exodus 17:15.
YHWH tsdqnwv 3072 (3068+6664)   = my right-ness, Jeremiah 23:6.
YHWH shlwvm 3073 (3068+7965)   = my peace, Judges 6:24.
YHWH shmh 3074 (3068+8033)   =   here with me, Ezekiel 48:35.
YHWH yowtham 3147 (3068+8535)   =   A perfect pair we are

There is an interesting one, that the crispy experts will never let you know. One that God calls Himself. Check this out in exactly the way He arranged the words in Hebrew because it is God speaking:
Genesis 17:1
"When was Abram old ninety years and nine years, and appeared the Lord unto Abram, and said unto him, I God[410] the Almighty[7706]; walk before me, and be perfect."

God 410 is Aleph, Lamed, which means 'Strong authority' and is defined as 'strength, hero'. In Hebrew it is Al. Almighty, 7706 is Sheen, Dalet, Hey, plural of the root word defined and used in Hebrew to signify the word 'breast' 7699 (Sheen, Dalet). So, 'the Almighty' is defined as 'The Breast is revealed'.

God calls Himself to us The revealed nurturer, Strong Hero. Al Shd. Think for a while on that ladies and gentlemen.

We don't need to have a problem with calling Him 'God' or calling Jesus 'Jesus' they are just the English language derivations of their names. They can hear you when you call Them. A rose by any other name is still a rose. I have a problem when we start calling a gun a rose, or start calling a rose a shoe. This is the case for such words as 'christian', 'church', 'praise', 'worship', 'holy', 'tithes and offerings', 'religion', 'spiritual', 'black people', 'white people', the 'human' 'race'. They are all socially engineered exercises in propaganda. Those who have an ear to hear will know.

Having looked at the defining characteristics of God, none describe an authority that sits back and watches. I do not believe man has yet been introduced to that being. In the bible we are given to know the Creator of the heavens and the earth. He is our sovereign authority. However, I believe that there is more to know.

For now, we have an Authority who is our authority, described by His etymology as having a feminine root, being plural and having all authority over people on earth. He has created us all and everything else out of chaos.

Putting all of these together, we can understand why Jesus called Him Father. He also requires us, for now in this dispensation of time to have Him only as our God. No other.

Other gods, including ourselves ("…Ye are gods;.." Psalm 82:6) can at best have only a piece of the story, and worst case scenario lead you to give up your soul to vanity which will eventually kill your spirit for good. That, my friends, is too dangerous a road to travel. You and the god of whatever, are no match for the great dragon. Revelation 12:9;

"And the great dragon was cast out, that old serpent, called the Devil, and Satan, which deceiveth the whole world: he was cast out into the earth, and his angels were cast out with him."

Knowing the God of Abraham Isaac and Jacob is essential if you want eternal peace and security. Knowing Him is also the essential ingredient needed in order to apprehend the Glory.

The bible says in Habakkuk 2:14;

"For the earth shall be filled with the knowledge of the glory of the Lord, as the waters cover the sea."

and Colossians 1:26,27;

"Even the mystery which hath been hid from ages and from generations, but now is made manifest to his saints: To whom God would make known what is the riches of the glory of this mystery among the Gentiles; which is Christ in you, the hope of glory:"

The mystery of all time on this planet it just that. You. Christ in us is the hope of glory. So let's break that down.

Christ = the anointing delivered by the anointed One, Jesus, to you.

You = a saint, a member of His body, a member of His Church and a disciple. Not a christian/crispy-one, there is no such thing as a christian.

Glory is 3519 in Strong's Hebrew and is the 'splendour' and 'copiousness' of God. The Hebrews remained in awe of God, often only dealing with the connotative meanings of God's characteristics rather than the denotative. In the Greek, 'glory' is given meaning in Strong's number 1391 which is a broader and wider application of its denotative root word 1380 which means 'an opinion'. So, glory means to broadcast the opinion of God.

That is what it is all about, Alfie. You have to let your heart lead the way. The anointing in you, in your spirit dearest men, is the hope this world has for good. Alfie, sadly does not let his heart lead the way and that is where we have the problem Houston. Males are not a creating vessel and so are often too mechanical in their outlook. Yet we are told that God made man in His own image, then separated them into male and female counterparts. So then, a bloke is the full image and likeness of God when standing next to his woman. Likewise a woman is the full image and likeness of God when standing beside her bloke. By the side and never behind. If she is behind, the man is unhedged as far as God is concerned. We women came out of the bloke to hedge his blessings and get him there. But where? you may well ask. God said in the garden of Eden that man looked amongst all the creatures that God created and there was no creature to be found that could be a 'help' for him. As we saw earlier the word help for Adam was 'to see the cut person'. Adam had not eaten of the tree of life, either then or now. The word for 'of life' is 'hchyym', Hey, Chet, Yood, Yood, Mem; which means to have full computation and ability in the perpetuation of the cycle of life, driven by the key element water, under our firmament. Had Adam had hachayyim, he would have understood the lifegiver that Eve was and would never have squealed on her. He would know she and he powered together can create their own universe systems. God took her out of him so he could begin to appreciate that power potential. We are in God's image, but He can create universes without needing to see the female section of Him cut out in front of Him.

So Alfie it's all about your heart; wherein is your woman. Yeah, the one God gave you, not the one you arbitrarily chose for yourself.

All Adam got, was of the tree of the knowledge of good (2896, 'ttwvb' Tet, Wav, Bet; Surrounding security of the house, 'cheer') and evil ('wru' Wav, Reysh, Ayin; Hook what the highest sees, 'adversity'). So he got knowledge of the joy and pain of life before he mastered what life even is.

So get to know your woman dude. God has His feminine nurturing love inside of Him. Same, same. You are gOD, small g yet big.

In the state of Adam being alone he had no power to look inside himself to see the (feminine) ability of nurturing and love and life. Eating from the tree of cheer and adversity would do him no good whilst he was alone, because he had limited power and understanding. He would be unable to exercise omnipresence and so would just in essence be a bi-polar mortal. If he ate from the tree of cheer and adversity, and the tree of eternal life and still couldn't see the eve inside him, he would just be eternal cannon fodder for the devil.

God sees and always operates as a dual force both male ('zkr' Zayin, Kaf, Reysh; The weapon that sustains the head) and female ('wvnqbh' Wav, Noon, Qoof, bet, Hey; The hook of life is revealed last from inside). Adam needed help to see the wvnqbh inside of him. So God gave him help ('uzr' Ayin, Zayin, Reysh; To see the cut person). All that 'help meet' stuff is a truck load of nonsense.

So, God cut her out so that the he-she could operate more excellently. So, now, we are going the other way around in order for God to perfect us as gods that are excellent enough to be able to overcome all evil. Having already been given knowledge of good and evil through the first man and woman, we are now to shape ourselves in righteousness to eat of everlasting life. It ain't no wonder that the angels were clueless as to why God created such a being. Right up until Jesus died. Then a funny thing happened on the way from the cross. As Jesus began to rise from the dead it dawned on all angels, both good and bad, that the tree of everlasting life had been obtained by a mortal and so the two components necessary in order to become like God had been apprehended. 1 Corinthians 2:6-8, Ephesians 3:9-11;
"Howbeit we speak wisdom among them that are perfect: yet not the wisdom of this world, nor of the princes of this world, that come to nought: But we speak the wisdom of God in a mystery, even the hidden wisdom, which God ordained before the world unto our glory: Which none of the princes of this world knew: for had they known it, they would not have crucified the Lord of glory."

"And to make all men see what is the fellowship of the mystery, which from the beginning of the world hath been hid in God, who

created all things by Jesus Christ: To the intent that now unto the principalities and powers in heavenly places might be known by the church the manifold wisdom of God, According to the eternal purpose which he purposed in Christ Jesus our Lord:.."

In addition to that unfolding masterful mystery, is the fact that God subjected the world to inutility, Romans 8:19-22;
"For the earnest expectation of the creature waiteth for the manifestation of the sons of God. For the creature was made subject to vanity[3153], not willingly, but by reason of him who hath subjected the same in hope, Because the creature itself also shall be delivered from the bondage of corruption into the glorious liberty of the children of God. For we know that the whole creation groaneth and travaileth in pain together until now."
3153 is from 3152 which means 'inutility'. We cannot use all of the planet, because at the moment we live on a flat plane covered by waters above a dome firmament, with waters below us in a domed sea. Just like God said He did it.

We live here and we leave here, most by way of the grave, where we are delivered out of this state. There, there are no more problems. Anyway, maybe more about that whole shape of the earth not being spherical thing in another book, for now Isaiah 40:22;
"It is he that sitteth upon the circle of the earth, and the inhabitants thereof are as grasshoppers; that stretcheth out the heavens as a curtain, and spreadeth them out as a tent to dwell in:"
(it was a sphere, before Adam and Eve arrived. It ain't one now).

Now to get a little bit Christopher Nolan on you, God did all of this thing, this planet, this creation to have the opportunity to fall in love. You can't fall in love unless one or both participants are subject to time. Einstein reckoned that we are already able to access time travel but that we are bound by gravity. However, gravity is not a force, in that, Einstein was correct. It is a relationship; relativity. That is how God designed it. The movements of our sun moon and stars are the result of God's weighing the mass and activity of sub atomic particles, then calculating how many of them and what permutation of them were needed for each thing He threw into existence. We are all linked to everything; relatively. God designed all as a potter throws his clay, Isaiah 40:12;

"Who hath measured the waters in the hollow of his hand, and meted out heaven with the span, and comprehended the dust of the earth in a measure, and weighed the mountains in scales, and the hills in a balance?"

The reason for the scope of this inutility was to ensure this painful process was contained enough so as not to cause eternal other solar system reaching damage via the perpetuation of evil and foolishness. As can be seen in Genesis chapter 1, Genesis was not the beginning. It was just the beginning for our world. Check out the ominous space between verses 1 and 2. What God must have created as good, and what must have happened to it after Lucifer was cast out of heaven. Some people call it 'gap theory', Genesis 1:1,2;

"1 In the beginning God created the heaven and the earth.
2 And the earth was without form, and void; and darkness was upon the face of the deep. And the Spirit of God moved upon the face of the waters."
So obviously something went wrong between verses 1 and 2. God always initiates His creations as good entities.

As women we should also be subject to the confines of this planet but God allows us to pull in spirits from His dwelling place. Unlike animals, only the womb of a woman can maintain the spiritual precedence necessary for God to adjust balances here on earth. Hence His ability to bring Jesus through Mary's womb in spite of all the disobedience that was rife in Israel. He has given us women the ability to self-perpetuate a life giving balance on this planet. Think about the confessions of Mary and her cousin Elizabeth. They kept the things that they said, thought and felt so clear and in line with the words that God told them that John jumped up in Elizabeth's womb when he heard Mary saying hello.

These crispy male doctors do not tell us much about the totally amazing thing that childbirth is. Did you know that there is a system in a pregnant woman's body called the 'cauda equina', so named because its form is like a horse's tail. This multiple stranded cord wraps itself around the womb and feeds intricate electrical and spiritual signals to the unborn child which inform it of every single feeling, thought and aspiration of its mother. How about the 'post partem? If the separation occurs, it will never close again.

As a woman, Sarah 'fenced' Abraham's blessing as discussed earlier. It is not possible to have a fence fencing an object with another fence around it and have only one private space. If there are two fences around one article then one fence is just fencing a fence, and creating a void space between the two fences. That is what happens when an uninformed man decides to Join himself to more than one woman. In actual fact, not only do the laws of 'fencing' indicate that it would all make much more sense if at all, the other way around, so that one fence was around multiple objects, but also the laws of nurturing a nation, the anatomy of man and woman and the laws of nature.

Abraham's father, Terah was called by God to leave Ur. Note that there is no mention of Terah's wives, they may have died along with one of their sons, Haran in Ur. I can imagine that things were not going too well there for the whole family, and God wanted them to leave. Terah took them and left for Canaan, but for some reason stopped in Haran. Perhaps his multiple wives were still alive and causing him too much grief. Too much void space. Genesis 11:31,32;
"And Terah took Abram his son, and Lot the son of Haran his son's son, and Sarai his daughter in law, his son Abram's wife; and they went forth with them from Ur of the Chaldees, to go into the land of Canaan; and they came unto Haran, and dwelt there. And the days of Terah were two hundred and five years: and Terah died in Haran."

From there, Abraham picked up the baton and because he had the holy singular two-made-one Join that God needed to pull this thing off, things began to go well for him. Abraham was not influenced by his father Terah as regards women. Even to the point where being offered another woman by his own wise wife and having a child with that woman because his wife told him to, did not quench his full devotion and commitment to only Sarah and the sure singular promise of God.

When things started to fall apart for Hagar, that other woman, God never had a word to say to her. God spoke to her only when she cast her son, the son of Abraham, into a bush. Hagar brought her own house down with her mouth, in ridiculing Sarah and Isaac. But God made room for her son Ishmael, blessed him and made him a nation.

Sarah misjudged the fact that not all women were like her. This nearly proved to be fatal for the promise of God in Abraham's life. Sarah was the type of woman who would probably go direct to God to ask what she needed to know in Eden about the tree.

God needed women like Sarah then and He needs them nowadays to realise that they are created for their own divine purpose. Men also are, however women are cut from a different cloth; from the side of that mixed male/female creation, which is the male. He was cut from the brown ground.

Had Sarah understood her own precedent, the enmity between 'christians' and 'muslims' would not exist today and Ishmael could still have been made a nation by another father. The nation of Islam is just that, a Nation. It is not a faith. God never intended it to be. How could it be? It is not possible to retrospectively declare the beginning of a system of faith if the subjects of your retrospection had no part in it or knowledge of it.

God intended Islam to be a collection of people worldwide who maintain the precepts of honour, learning and the spiritual wisdom people of this planet need in order to run it in a Godly manner; particularly to combat the injustices perpetrated by evil twisted men. Thankfully, due to such individuals as Drew Ali and Rahm Emmanuel we are now finally getting somewhere with that premise.

The language spoken in Judea and the surrounding areas by Israelites whilst Jesus was alive was Aramaic. So Jesus would have said 'As salaam alaikum', not 'Shalom'. Let us stop with the fallacy of division and get on with the plan and purposes of God, not somebody else's stupid religious agenda.

There is no such word as 'religion', as pertains to any kind of Godly life. There is also no such word as 'worship'. The word 'religion' is a fake word covering a real meaning. The word 'worship' is a real word given a fake meaning. Let's deal with 'religion' first.

The concept of religion as a term was coined by the Romans when they were attempting to become equal with God and the gods in their deification of Nero following the death of Jesus and the persecution of the early Church. Nero probably chose to call himself Nero for reasons of authentication that would have appeared obvious in the demographic at that time. The whole of the Roman Empire was and still is a fake system superimposing itself on what it hopes, is largely a defenceless proletariat. Those among the proletariat noble enough to stand up for what they know to be right are undesirables, like Jesus. The word religion literally means re (back to) legion (bondage). That is all. And that is what it is. An attempt to nip all the power of the early Church in the bud.

Every 'religious' offering from Rome was and is merely a dearth to take you back to bondage hook line and sinker. Mary said nothing about needing to pray to her or being the way to salvation. Jesus on the other hand repeatedly asserted that He was the Way, so why pray to Mary? Jesus is not busy doing something else for some other planet. If Jesus is eagerly awaiting the Church to make His enemies His footstool, why would He not speed that up by being the recipient of the prayers of righteous men and women? It is our God and Father who then answers them.

It's ridiculous. Even a child can comprehend that there is no logic in praying to Mary. On top of that, the bible says we are to come boldly to the throne of grace, Hebrews 4:14-16;

"Seeing then that we have a great high priest, that is passed into the heavens, Jesus the Son of God, let us hold fast our profession. For we have not an high priest which cannot be touched with the feeling of our infirmities; but was in all points tempted like as we are, yet without sin. Let us therefore come boldly unto the throne of grace, that we may obtain mercy, and find grace to help in time of need."

The whole catholic thing is anathema.

The word religion is only used in the new contract, which should already have you suspicious as to what the equivalent word was for 'religion' in the Old Testament. The Greek word for religion is 'thréskeia' Strong's number 2356 and means 'worship'. So then the task is to find out what the word 'worship' is in the Old Testament, and there you have your true word and meaning, which the word 'religion' usurped and replaced.

In Genesis 29:35 Leah gives birth to a child;

"And she conceived again, and bare a son: and she said, Now will I praise the Lord: therefore she called his name Judah; and left bearing."

The word 'Judah' is Strong's number 3063 'Yhwvdh' and is from the root word 3034 'awvdh'. Awvdh means '…hold out the hand…to revere or worship with extended hands'. If you remember, this is what Paul said the Corinthian men were failing to do.

So, 'religion' means to throw out your hands, celebrate and 'worship' the God of Abraham, Isaac and Jacob. Being 'religious' means to be like Judah. Judaism. Simple.
Incidentally, one of the real names for 'God' as mentioned earlier is YHWH or Yhwvh. If you look at the Hebrew words for Yhwvh and Judah next to each other, they are very similar and quickly tell you the plan for redemption. YHWH = Yhwvh = Yood, Hey, Wav, Hey; The hand that reveals the secure nail of revelation. YHWDH = Yhwvdh = Judah = worship = Yood, Hey, Wav, Dalet, Hey; The hand that reveals the secure nail gives a door to revelation.

So now we comprehend what the real meaning is behind the fake words in this context; 'worship' and 'religion'. They both mean Judaism as a way in to God, i.e., through the door which is the seed of Abraham which is our Yhwvsu (Jesus Christ).

There are not hundreds of religions on the planet from which we are all in a quandary as to what to choose. That is a stream of babble. Every practice outside of the God of Abraham Isaac and Jacob is a cultural social club – and that's okay, some of us need social clubs. However, many of these other 'religions' are actually a part of God's story. For example, God told Jacob in Genesis 32:28 that his new name was Israel. These syllables would not be unfamiliar to Jacob. Egypt was the dominant civilization at that time and its citizens worshiped Isis and Ra, Is-Ra-El would sound familiar. As mentioned earlier, God is called Horus in 2 Chronicles 28:3. The image of the mother and child in that story predates Mary and Jesus. However, we finally got some closure and thanks to the diligence of his mother against all odds, Jesus was born to us and the grand plan is now finally afoot. Thank you Jesus. Nobody does it better.
Think about Melchizedek, 'King of Peace', whom Abraham paid homage to, Hebrews 7:1-6;

"For this Melchisedec, king of Salem, priest of the most high God, who met Abraham returning from the slaughter of the kings, and blessed him; To whom also Abraham gave a tenth part of all; first being by interpretation King of righteousness, and after that also King of Salem, which is, King of peace; Without father, without

mother, without descent, having neither beginning of days, nor end of life; but made like unto the Son of God; abideth a priest continually. Now consider how great this man was, unto whom even the patriarch Abraham gave the tenth of the spoils. And verily they that are of the sons of Levi, who receive the office of the priesthood, have a commandment to take tithes of the people according to the law, that is, of their brethren, though they come out of the loins of Abraham: But he whose descent is not counted from them received tithes of Abraham, and blessed him that had the promises."

Same Spirit of Peace that is Jesus, just an earlier manifestation. Even the literal force behind the words that God speaks; because Jesus is the Word made flesh, same spirit, previous manifestation.

We don't know how long this earth has been in operation as a life bearing entity. As mentioned, there is a big gap in Genesis. We are now hearing of alluvial deposits in the Grand Canyon that predate all of our history, and about a people called the 'Sumerians' who predated Egypt by millennia. Maybe all sorts of crazy happened with them, evil ran amock and God had to wait until He was legal, step in, close off the planet with a dome, put life giving water atop and bottom, confine the evil, rinse and repeat.

Although it seems that no God should remove nations, when evil became the norm in the Old Testament, in order to prevent the same chaos, death and post apocalyptic mess from occurring He had to remove those nations in order to give genetic room for Jesus to arrive. Now that Jesus is with us, no need to colonise and kill in the name of God anymore. The civilising element has been born to us and completed His task to the fullness. So whom ever performs the task of killing in the name of God since Jesus rose from the dead is a liar.

I call this thing we are in, a succession of 'rinse and repeat'. When things fail, and God cannot get creation to sustain itself in light, atom and brown earth, we all go into the washing cycle again. Well, this time Jesus came and He got it right because He is God's son and He is The undertaker for all evil. He has full light, atom and brown earth in Him. So when we get into Him, we become the righteousness of God.

Some have believed in an essence of Jesus Christ all of their lives, and when they die they will say to God, 'Oh, was that essence I believed 'Jesus', God will say 'yes'. Done deal; they're in. All the while these crispyones/christians are playing word games and culture exchange musical chairs, pretending that going forth missionaryising, terrorising and crusading peoples and nations has anything to do with a righteous God. Romans 10:11;

"For the scripture saith, Whosoever believeth on him shall not be ashamed."

The wisdom is to determine what of our history on this planet is part of God's agenda; that God of Abraham Isaac and Jacob, and what is at best mere imitation. Really, it is not so difficult to tell.

So now that we know 'religion' means 'worship' which is Judaism, what does worship mean? Well, saying 'let us worship' is like saying 'let us Olympics'. Which discipline do you want to partake in? Throwing a javelin, running the 800 metres, Judo, freestyle swimming, gymnastic floor exercise…what? They are all very different. The thing they share in common is that if you do any of them on a regular basis or even once, they are health to you.

Here are some of the things that worship is.

Genesis 22:5

"And Abraham said unto his young men, Abide ye here with the ass; and I and the lad will go yonder and worship, and come again to you."

Nshchhwvh – Noon, Sheen, Chet, Hey, Wav, Hey; 'Life is devoured by separating the security of revelation'.

So, laying down a valuable life.

Genesis 24:26

"And the man bowed down his head, and worshipped the Lord."

Yshchhwv – Yood, Sheen, Chet, Hey, Wav; 'The hand that devours the separation is revealed and secured'.

So, the thing of most importance and value is now a weight off my shoulders.

Exodus 24:1

"And he said unto Moses, Come up unto the Lord, thou, and Aaron, Nadab, and Abihu, and seventy of the elders of Israel; and worship ye afar off."

Hshchhwvychm – Hey, Sheen, Chet, Hey, Wav, Yood, Chet, Mem; 'Behold the teeth that separate the revelation, the security of the work of life'.

So, understand that God will do the mighty work through a chosen person.

And here are some meanings for 'praise';

Exodus 15:11
"Who is like unto thee, O Lord, among the gods? who is like thee, glorious in holiness, fearful in praises, doing wonders?"
Thlt – 8416, defined as '…a song…connotes genuine appreciation for the great actions or the character of its object' from the verb hll 1984 ('halal', we are kin to the sons of Ishmael), defined as 'to be clear of sound but usually of colour…to shine…commend…boast…could also be to shout'. Incidentally, halal is Hey, Lamed, Lamed; 'Behold the authority of the authority'. So, what makes God God, brings a shining vibe to your heart.

Leviticus 19:24
"But in the fourth year all the fruit thereof shall be holy to praise the Lord withal"
Hlwvl – 1974, defined as 'a celebration of thanksgiving…' again from the verb 'halal'.
So, have a party to celebrate Him.

Judges 5:2
"Praise ye the Lord for the avenging of Israel, when the people willingly offered themselves."
Brk – 1288 meaning, what issues from the covered son (the prince). Mostly blessings but also sometimes a curse. So, our benefit from acknowledging His majesty.

2 Samuel 22:50
"Therefore I will give thanks unto thee, O Lord, among the heathen, and I will sing praises unto thy name."
Zmr – 2167 defined as 'to make music…through striking with the fingers'
So, grab your guitar.

2 Chronicles 7:3
"And when all the children of Israel saw how the fire came down, and the glory of the Lord upon the house, they bowed themselves with their faces to the ground upon the pavement, and

worshipped, and praised the Lord, saying, For he is good; for his mercy endureth for ever."

You can see from the above text that worship does not mean bowing down. Otherwise it would say 'they worshipped with their faces to the ground upon the pavement, and worshipped, and praised the Lord, saying…'

Hwvdwvt – not satisfactorily assigned 3034 (Ydh) 'to acknowledge…to use the hand…to extend the hand…' Hwvdwvt is Hey, Wav, Dalet, Wav, Tav; 'Revealed, the secure door securing the covenant'.

So, come on in.

I am sure there are many more.

There is no such thing as a christian, as signifies a disciple, especially in the eyes of God. So stop calling yourself one. The term was coined by some people in Antioch who were not believers and then Peter used the term once. Christian denotes one who has *something like* The Anointing. That does not mean anything in particular, and so gives licence to any fool who says they are a christian to hang innocent people from trees, rape, pillage, enslave and steal in the name of their christian nothingness. Basically 'christian' just means 'I have garnered myself with my own authority, cloaked in a falsehood that I have a god given license to do as I determine is necessary for a means to my chosen ends'. We are told in the bible of a similar pattern in John 10:10;

"The thief cometh not, but for to steal, and to kill, and to destroy:.."

so, Matthew 7:20;

"Wherefore by their fruits ye shall know them."

Do not align yourself with such people. They are the biggest crew of thieves, murderers and annihilators that the world has ever seen. The word 'christian' is mentioned in the bible 3 times. The word 'disciple' is mentioned 267 times on my last count. I suggest that you spread good news, call yourself a disciple, and make disciples like Jesus said and stop toying with that empty word. Making christians and killing nations is not the same thing.

The people that God has desired to see from the beginning of creation are people of faith, Hebrews 11:1;

"Now faith is the substance of things hoped for, the evidence of things not seen."
The substance of things hoped for and the evidence of things yet unseen is the creative word of God, Genesis 1:3;
"And God said, Let there be light: and there was light."

John 1:1-14 abridged.
"In the beginning was the Word, and the Word was with God, and the Word was God. The same was in the beginning with God. All things were made by him; and without him was not any thing made that was made...And the Word was made flesh, and dwelt among us, (and we beheld his glory, the glory as of the only begotten of the Father,) full of grace and truth."
Therefore Faith = Jesus. Anyone professing to be a child of God must show Jesus' attributes through their own personality. Before Miriam knew the ten commandments or how to behave as a covenant woman, by faith she hid Moses in a basket. She knew that the Hebrews bore close resemblance to the Egyptians and subsequently an Egyptian princess claimed that Moses was her son.

In due course, the law came through Moses and the Hebrews left Egypt with additional non-Hebrew people who could see a better life for themselves with the Hebrews than that which they had in Egypt. These additions first became proselytes and then became Jews. Jews, not Hebrews and not Israelites. Exodus 12:38, Numbers 11:1-5;
"And a mixed multitude went up also with them; and flocks, and herds, even very much cattle."

"And when the people complained, it displeased the Lord: and the Lord heard it; and his anger was kindled; and the fire of the Lord burnt among them, and consumed them that were in the uttermost parts of the camp...And the mixt multitude that was among them fell a lusting: and the children of Israel also wept again, and said, Who shall give us flesh to eat? We remember the fish, which we did eat in Egypt freely; the cucumbers, and the melons, and the leeks, and the onions, and the garlick:..."
I doubt that many of the Israelites had garlic and hors d'oeuvres to eat as slaves in Egypt, even when Moses (Moshe) was in charge. It was the 'additions' that initiated the complaining, but it was all that fell dead in the wilderness save Joshua.

58

God did not seem to have much of a problem with His people until they became mixed with converts to Judaism. In those early days of mixing, those newly converted in the exodus from Egypt stayed on the outside of the habitation. One has to wonder if they harboured the right motive of conversion in light of the many riches Israel left Egypt with. However, leaven leavens the whole lump. The Hebrews also encountered problems with the converts regarding money, usary (interest rates) and a return to bondage, Nehemiah 5:1-12;

"And there was a great cry of the people and of their wives against their brethren the Jews. For there were that said, We, our sons, and our daughters, are many: therefore we take up corn for them, that we may eat, and live. Some also there were that said, We have mortgaged our lands, vineyards, and houses, that we might buy corn, because of the dearth. There were also that said, We have borrowed money for the king's tribute, and that upon our lands and vineyards. Yet now our flesh is as the flesh of our brethren, our children as their children: and, lo, we bring into bondage our sons and our daughters to be servants, and some of our daughters are brought unto bondage already: neither is it in our power to redeem them; for other men have our lands and vineyards. And I was very angry when I heard their cry and these words. Then I consulted with myself, and I rebuked the nobles, and the rulers, and said unto them, Ye exact usury, every one of his brother. And I set a great assembly against them...Restore, I pray you, to them, even this day, their lands, their vineyards, their oliveyards, and their houses, also the hundredth part of the money, and of the corn, the wine, and the oil, that ye exact of them. Then said they, We will restore them, and will require nothing of them; so will we do as thou sayest. Then I called the priests, and took an oath of them, that they should do according to this promise."

So if you see a Jewish person who is a banker charging interest then they have not kept the faith. The love of money is the root of all evil.

Thankfully, people do convert for noble reasons as sincere children of God, Esther 8:17, Ruth 1:16;

"...the Jews had joy and gladness, a feast and a good day. And many of the people of the land became Jews; for the fear of the Jews fell upon them."

"...for whither thou goest, I will go; and where thou lodgest, I will lodge: thy people shall be my people, and thy God my God:"

Everyone in the congregation then and now is accepted of God by promise. However, there remain foundational activities that can only be carried out by those who are of Hebrew origin/Israelite bloodline, Numbers 16:39,40;

"And Eleazar the priest took the brasen censers, wherewith they that were burnt had offered; and they were made broad plates for a covering of the altar: To be a memorial unto the children of Israel, that no stranger, which is not of the seed of Aaron, come near to offer incense before the Lord; that he be not as Korah, and as his company: as the Lord said to him by the hand of Moses."

Still today, there are foundational activities and decisions that can only be performed by the righteous, Jeremiah 34:2-5, Proverbs 29:1, 2;
"...Behold, I will give this city into the hand of the king of Babylon, and he shall burn it with fire: And thou shalt not escape out of his hand,... Yet hear the word of the Lord, O Zedekiah king of Judah; Thus saith the Lord of thee, Thou shalt not die by the sword: But thou shalt die in peace: and with the burnings of thy fathers,..."

"He, that being often reproved hardeneth his neck, shall suddenly be destroyed, and that without remedy. When the righteous are in authority, the people rejoice: but when the wicked beareth rule, the people mourn."

We are in mourning on this planet. If you don't believe me, check out the number of children that go missing in the United Kingdom every day. Then check out the number of children that go missing in the United States of America every day. It is more than mourning.
It is a state of emergency.
The numbers are 400 in the U.K and 800 in the U.S.A. If you are not ready for some urgent change then you should be. Nothing at all is going on here until we sort this mess out. We need to be able to call upon the original Hebrews and the righteous to initiate change. There is nothing of any importance happening here on this planet until we sort this out. Jesus says;
"...'without me ye can do nothing'." John 15:5

By the time of Jesus' birth the congregation of Hebrews and converts/proselytes was entirely mixed. In the new contract we see that there are different ways that the noun 'Jews' is spelt to represent this. Unfortunately, these 'experts' have translated all of these as the same word with the same Strong's Greek number 2453. However, Jesus is Hebrew and had a lot of run ins with 'Jews', so it stands to reason that this great book we have access to would spell out the differentiating revelation. Everything is maths.

We have the adjectives: 'joudaion', 'joudaious/joudaiois', or 'joudaioi' all translated as the noun 'Jews'. I have no clue of the Greek language and have no inkling to find out what these words mean etymologically. However, I can read, and have a brain that works.

Every time the bible mentions the word joudaion, they are faithful Jews. Every time the bible mentions the word joudaioi, they are faithless Jews. Every time the bible mentions the word joudaious/joudaiois, they are a mixture of Jews. So bear with me while I break it down.

1. joudaion

Matthew 2:2, Matthew 27:11, Matthew 27:29, Mark 15:2, Mark 15:9, Mark 15:12, Mark 15:18, Mark 15:26, Luke 7:3, Luke 23:3, Luke 23:37, Luke 23:38, Luke 23:51, John 2:6, John 2:13, John 3:1, John 4:22, John 5:1, John 6:4, John 7:2, John 7:13, John 11:19, John 11:45, John 11:55, John 12:9, John 12:11, John 18:12, John 18:33, John 18:39, John 19:3, John 19:19, John 19:20, John 19:21, John 19:38, John 19:42, John 20:19, Acts 10:22, Acts 10:39, Acts 12:11, Acts 13:5, Acts 13:43, Acts 14:1, Acts 14:5, Acts 17:1, Acts 17:10, Acts 18:2, Acts 19:13, Acts 19:33, Acts 20:3, Acts 20:19, Acts 22:12, Acts 22:30, Acts 23:27, Acts 25:2, Acts 25:8, Acts 25:15, Acts 25:24, Acts 26:2, Acts 28:17, Acts 28:19, Romans 3:29, Romans 9:24, 2 Corinthians 11:24, 1 Thessalonians 2:14.

2. joudaious/joudaiois

Matthew 28:15, John 4:9, John 5:15, John 8:31, John 9:22, John 10:19, John 11:33, John 11:54, John 13:33, John 18:14, John 18:35, John 18:36, John 18:38, John 19:14, John 19:40, Acts 9:22, Acts 11:19, Acts 12:3, Acts 14:4, Acts 16:3, Acts 17:17, Acts 18:4, Acts 18:5, Acts 18:14, Acts 18:19, Acts 18:28, Acts 19:10, Acts 19:17, Acts 19:34, Acts 20:21, Acts 21:20, Acts 21:21, Acts 21:39, Acts 22:3, Acts 24:5, Acts 24:9, Acts 24:27, Acts 25:9, Acts 25:10, Acts 26:3, Romans 3:9, 1 Corinthians 1:23, 1

Corinthians 1:24, 1 Corinthians 9:20, 1 Corinthians 10:32, Revelation 2:9, Revelation 3:9.

3. joudaioi
Mark 7:3, John 1:19, John 2:18, John 2:20, John 5:10, John 5:16, John 5:18, John 6:41, John 6:52, John 7:1, John 7:11, John 7:15, John 7:35, John 8:22, John 8:48, John 8:52, John 8:57, John 9:18, John 10:24, John 10:31, John 10:33, John 11:8, John 11:31, John 11:36, John 18:20, John 18:31, John 19:7, John 19:12, John 19:31, acts 2:5, Acts 2:10, Acts 9:23, Acts 13:45, Acts 13:50, Acts 14:2, Acts 14:19, Acts 16:20, Acts 17:5, Acts 17:13, Acts 18:12, Acts 21:11, Acts 21:27, Acts 23:12, Acts 23:20, Acts 24:18, Acts 25:7, Acts 26:4, Acts 26:21, Acts 28:29, 1 Corinthians 1:22, 1 Corinthians 12:13, Galatians 2:13, Galatians 2:15.

1. joudaion
Each instance of joudaion in the bible is about a good bunch of Jews. Here are some interesting instances to point out.

Matthew 2:1,2;
"Now when Jesus was born in Bethlehem of Judaea in the days of Herod the king, behold, there came wise men from the east to Jerusalem, Saying, Where is he that is born King of the Jews[2453] joudaion? for we have seen his star in the east, and are come to worship him."

John 11:44-46;
"And he that was dead came forth, bound hand and foot with graveclothes: and his face was bound about with a napkin. Jesus saith unto them, Loose him, and let him go. Then many of the Jews[2453]joudaion which came to Mary, and had seen the things which Jesus did, believed on him. But some of them went their ways to the Pharisees, and told them what things Jesus had done."
Not everybody at Lazurus' funeral were the good guys. But those who believed in Jesus separated themselves as the faithful. The bad guys were so bad that they actually wanted to re-kill Lazarus because of the people who believed on Jesus as a result of his resurrection.
John 12:10,11;
"But the chief priests consulted that they might put Lazarus also to death; Because that by reason of him many of the Jews[2453]joudaion went away, and believed on Jesus."

John 7:12,13;

"And there was much murmuring among the people concerning him: for some said, He is a good man: others said, Nay; but he deceiveth the people. Howbeit no man spake openly of him for fear of the Jews[2453]joudaion."

This tells us that the faithful Jews were a force to be reckoned with at that point. The faithless Jews would not care about people discussing Jesus.

Luke 7:2,3;

"And a certain centurion's servant, who was dear unto him, was sick, and ready to die. And when he heard of Jesus, he sent unto him the elders of the Jews[2453]joudaion, beseeching him that he would come and heal his servant."

John 3:1;

"There was a man of the Pharisees, named Nicodemus, a ruler of the Jews[2453]joudaion:.."

Most of the people chosen by the people to be in authority were good guys. Even though they were sometimes instructed to do bad things.

John 18:12;

"Then the band and the captain and officers of the Jews[2453]joudaion took Jesus, and bound him,"

However when Jesus was murdered on the cross those among the chief priests who had believed Him, not understanding the glory to come wanted to disassociate themselves from Him.

John 19:38;

"And after this Joseph of Arimathaea, being a disciple of Jesus, but secretly for fear of the Jews[2453]joudaion, besought Pilate that he might take away the body of Jesus: and Pilate gave him leave. He came therefore, and took the body of Jesus."

John 20:19;

"Then the same day at evening, being the first day of the week, when the doors were shut where the disciples were assembled for fear of the Jews[2453]joudaion, came Jesus and stood in the midst, and saith unto them, Peace be unto you."

John 19:21;

"Then said the chief priests of the Jews[2453]joudaion to Pilate, Write not, The King of the Jews; but that he said, I am King of the Jews."

A faithless chief priest would have just asked for the sign to be taken down if they didn't like it, anyhow, the sign read;

John 19:19;

"...Jesus Of Nazareth The King Of The Jews[2453]joudaion."

All of His disciples but one fled and left Him for dead. Thank God that Mary, John, Mary and Martha stayed by his side.

After Paul had killed Stephen, many believers found him guilty of murder and were suspicious of his conversion. They wanted him tried for murder.

Acts 20:3,19;

"And there abode three months. And when the Jews[2453]joudaion laid wait for him, as he was about to sail into Syria, he purposed to return through Macedonia."

"Serving the Lord with all humility of mind, and with many tears, and temptations, which befell me by the lying in wait of the Jews[2453]joudaion:.."

Acts 22:30;

"On the morrow, because he would have known the certainty wherefore he was accused of the Jews[2453]joudaion,.."

Acts 25:2,15,24;

"Then the high priest and the chief of the Jews[2453]joudaion informed him against Paul, and besought him,"

"About whom, when I was at Jerusalem, the chief priests and the elders of the Jews[2453]joudaion informed me, desiring to have judgment against him."

"...ye see this man, about whom all the multitude of the Jews[2453]joudaion have dealt with me, both at Jerusalem, and also here, crying that he ought not to live any longer."

The only multitude of Jews who would be crying for judgment and for Paul to die would be believers who didn't believe that he had really changed. Faithless Jews of a multitude would have no emphatic wish for Paul either way and could perhaps think Paul a benefit for baiting a trap for the early Church.

Acts 26:2-7;

"I think myself happy, king Agrippa, because I shall answer for myself this day before thee touching all the things whereof I am accused of the Jews[2453]joudaion: Especially because I know thee to be expert in all customs and questions which are among the Jews[2453]*joudaious*: wherefore I beseech thee to hear me patiently. My manner of life from my youth, which was at the first among mine own nation at Jerusalem, know all the Jews[2453]*joudaioi*; Which knew me from the beginning, if they would testify, that

after the most straitest sect of our religion I lived a Pharisee. And now I stand and am judged for the hope of the promise made of God, unto our fathers: Unto which promise our twelve tribes, instantly serving God day and night, hope to come. For which hope's sake, king Agrippa, I am accused of the Jews[2453]joudaion." Acts 28:17-19;

"And it came to pass, that after three days Paul called the chief of the Jews[2453]joudaion together: and when they were come together, he said unto them, Men and brethren, though I have committed nothing against the people, or customs of our fathers, yet was I delivered prisoner from Jerusalem into the hands of the Romans. Who, when they had examined me, would have let me go, because there was no cause of death in me. But when the Jews[2453]joudaion spake against it, I was constrained to appeal unto Caesar; not that I had ought to accuse my nation of."

Wow. That says it all. Poor Paul, nightmare life and an unhelpful ex wife. Nightmare.

The faithful had lost their way. If we are to understand the writings of Josephus, John was being chased from pillar to post with many unsuccessful assassinations against him, finally ending up imprisoned on the island of Patmos to write Revelation. Stephen and other leaders of the early Church had been killed by Paul before his conversion on the Damascus road. With no strong leader to guide them, it probably took some time before Peter mustered himself to the cause, Galatians 2:11-13;

"But when Peter was come to Antioch, I withstood him to the face, because he was to be blamed. For before that certain came from James, he did eat with the Gentiles: but when they were come, he withdrew and separated himself, fearing them which were of the circumcision. And the other Jews[2453]*joudaioi* dissembled likewise with him; insomuch that Barnabas also was carried away with their dissimulation."

The believers who were upset regarding the murder of Stephen decided to exact their own judgement upon Paul. Had they been unbelieving Jews they would not have wanted to kill Paul for murdering Stephen and all the other members of the early Church. Had these unbelieving Jews wanted to stop Paul in his apparent change of allegiance and his strengthening of the church, then they would have him brought up on murder chargers and attempted to put him to death also. So it must have been the believing Jews, 2 Corinthians 11:24;

"Of the Jews[2453]joudaion five times received I forty stripes save one."
1 Thessalonians 2:14;
"For ye, brethren, became followers of the churches of God which in Judaea are in Christ Jesus: for ye also have suffered like things of your own countrymen, even as they have of the Jews[2453]joudaion:"

That was the last use of the word joudaion in the bible. What God wants us to do now is forget this 'going to church' nonsense. If you need a social club of your peers, do that on your own time and stop calling it church. We need the Church from God. What is the difference? Judaism. Judaism equals taking care of widows and orphans, that is the difference. If your gathering on a Sunday does not financially support believing women who have lost their husbands through death or unbelief then it is not a church gathering. Men in the same circumstances do not need help, Proverbs 18:22;
"Whoso findeth a wife findeth a good thing, and obtaineth favour of the Lord."

It also needs to have reputable homes where orphans/looked after children are taken good Godly care of. And that is it voila you have Church.
Now, the catholics do an ungodly turn on this by declaring women barren and husbandless as nuns and abominations which cannot be written about concerning children. We must stop this insanity and the monopoly they think they have on the orchestration and voice of the power of God.

Let us stop playing 'church', read what God actually says in the bible through appropriate scholarly intellectual study of His Word and restore this planet to its former glory.

2. joudaious/joudaiois
Each instance of joudaious/joudaiois in the bible is about a mixed bunch of Jews. Here are some interesting instances of those words.

John 8:31;

"Then said Jesus to those Jews[2453]joudaious which believed on him, If ye continue in my word, then are ye my disciples indeed;"
You must continue in order to qualify.
John 10:18-21;
"No man taketh it from me, but I lay it down of myself. I have power to lay it down, and I have power to take it again. This commandment have I received of my Father. There was a division therefore again among the Jews[2453]joudaiois for these sayings. And many of them said, He hath a devil, and is mad; why hear ye him? Others said, These are not the words of him that hath a devil. Can a devil open the eyes of the blind?"
Acts 14:1-5;
"And it came to pass in Iconium, that they went both together into the synagogue of the Jews[2453]*joudaion*, and so spake, that a great multitude both of the Jews[2453]*joudaion* and also of the Greeks believed. But the unbelieving Jews[2453]*joudaioi* stirred up the Gentiles, and made their minds evil affected against the brethren. Long time therefore abode they speaking boldly in the Lord, which gave testimony unto the word of his grace, and granted signs and wonders to be done by their hands. But the multitude of the city was divided: and part held with the Jews[2453]joudaiois, and part with the apostles. And when there was an assault made both of the Gentiles, and also of the Jews[2453]*joudaion* with their rulers, to use them despitefully, and to stone them,"
It really was a struggle that we need to understand in these last days.
Revelation 2:9, 3:9;
"I know thy works, and tribulation, and poverty, (but thou art rich) and I know the blasphemy of them which say they are Jews[2453]joudaious, and are not, but are the synagogue of Satan."

"Behold, I will make them of the synagogue of Satan, which say they are Jews[2453]joudaious, and are not, but do lie; behold, I will make them to come and worship before thy feet, and to know that I have loved thee."
So why does it say 'mixed' here and not just 'faithful' Jews? Because most of our fight as believers is with the idiots in the mix who are crispyones/christians. They know they are stalling and attempting to leaven the whole lump. They would not dare call themselves disciples of Jesus because they have none of His attributes. These idiots are confusing those who aught to be saved and preventing the whole world from entering in to God through Jesus Christ. It is time we called them

out and removed ourselves from that unclean thing called christianity with its myriad of denominations.

1 Corinthians 1:24;

"But unto them which are called, both Jews[2453]joudaiois and Greeks, Christ the power of God, and the wisdom of God."

This helps us to understand what Jesus said in Matthew 22:14, "For many are called, but few are chosen."

3. joudaioi

Each instance of joudaioi in the bible is about the bad guys.

John 2:20;

"Then said the Jews[2453]joudaioi, Forty and six years was this temple in building, and wilt thou rear it up in three days?"

Always wanting an argument.

John 5:10,16,18;

"The Jews[2453]joudaioi therefore said unto him that was cured, It is the sabbath day: it is not lawful for thee to carry thy bed."

"And therefore did the Jews[2453]joudaioi persecute Jesus, and sought to slay him, because he had done these things on the sabbath day."

"Therefore the Jews[2453]joudaioi sought the more to kill him, because he not only had broken the sabbath, but said also that God was his Father, making himself equal with God."

Acts 2:5-13;

"And there were dwelling at Jerusalem Jews[2453]joudaioi, devout men, out of every nation under heaven. Now when this was noised abroad, the multitude came together, and were confounded, because that every man heard them speak in his own language...Phrygia, and Pamphylia, in Egypt, and in the parts of Libya about Cyrene, and strangers of Rome, Jews[2453]joudaioi and proselytes, Cretes and Arabians, we do hear them speak in our tongues the wonderful works of God. And they were all amazed, and were in doubt, saying one to another, What meaneth this? Others mocking said, These men are full of new wine."

It was only the proselytes (foreign converts to Judaism), Cretes and Arabians, who responded to Peter's teaching whilst the pious Jews mocked.

Acts 13:45,50;

"But when the Jews[2453]joudaioi saw the multitudes, they were filled with envy, and spake against those things which were spoken by Paul, contradicting and blaspheming."

"But the Jews[2453]joudaioi stirred up the devout and honourable women, and the chief men of the city, and raised persecution against Paul and Barnabas, and expelled them out of their coasts."
Acts 17:5,13;

"But the Jews[2453]joudaioi which believed not, moved with envy, took unto them certain lewd fellows of the baser sort, and gathered a company, and set all the city on an uproar, and assaulted the house of Jason, and sought to bring them out to the people."

"But when the Jews[2453]joudaioi of Thessalonica had knowledge that the word of God was preached of Paul at Berea, they came thither also, and stirred up the people."
Acts 21:11,27;

"And when he was come unto us, he took Paul's girdle, and bound his own hands and feet, and said, Thus saith the Holy Ghost, So shall the Jews[2453]joudaioi at Jerusalem bind the man that owneth this girdle, and shall deliver him into the hands of the Gentiles."

"And when the seven days were almost ended, the Jews[2453]joudaioi which were of Asia, when they saw him in the temple, stirred up all the people, and laid hands on him,"
Men of no honour who like to get others to do their bidding.
Acts 14:1,2;

"And it came to pass in Iconium, that they went both together into the synagogue of the Jews[2453]*joudaion*, and so spake, that a great multitude both of the Jews[2453]*joudaion* and also of the Greeks believed. But the unbelieving Jews[2453]joudaioi stirred up the Gentiles, and made their minds evil affected against the brethren."
We see in this scripture that it is clear who the joudaioi are.
Acts 25:7;

"And when he was come, the Jews[2453]joudaioi which came down from Jerusalem stood round about, and laid many and grievous complaints against Paul, which they could not prove."
No honour, rhyme or reason.
Acts 26:4;

"My manner of life from my youth, which was at the first among mine own nation at Jerusalem, know all the Jews[2453]joudaioi;"
Paul says that he used to roll with the bad guys.
1 Corinthians 12:13;

"For by one Spirit are we all baptized into one body, whether we be Jews[2453]joudaioi or Gentiles, whether we be bond or free; and have been all made to drink into one Spirit."

Paul humbly speaks about his own conversion from bad to good here.

It had been many generations since the days of the High Priest Eleazar, mentioned earlier. Now we see above that those in ministration to God *on the behalf of people* are mixed. And that actually sums up the need we had for Jesus to come to us as a man; in order to minister to us as our continual High Priest; never being mixed, so we have no doubts. Those in ministration *on the behalf of God* can never be mixed as those people are prophets, and if what they say is rubbish we all know they are not prophets.

What we all need to do now if we say we are believers is to filter out the rubbish, and discover the way to discern between the good and the bad. God wants to work through the lives of people of faith. Whether they are Hebrew or whether they are not. Faith as I have suggested is Jesus. It is astounding to find out through the study of the use of the word 'Jews' in the new contract that Paul had so much adversity from believers. In addition, the fact that the ministration to the joudaion Jews was so lacking. That suggests a need for a strong refreshing in the last days geared towards these Jews. Who are these Jews? They are the Hebrews who were visibly not gentiles. Those believers have not yet to this day had their innings of revelatory teaching regarding their status and their specific purpose in the last days except in the book of Revelation, 7:4;

"And I heard the number of them which were sealed: and there were sealed an hundred and forty and four thousand of all the tribes of the children of Israel."

The men above, virgins, will essentially be a group who have hair like Jesus, and skin like Jesus. I believe that God has begun the process of calling such people forth with the declaration given by Rahm Emanuel, Mayor of Chicago on 22nd December 2011.

God divorced Israel in Jeremiah 3:1-25 abridged;

"They say, If a man put away his wife, and she go from him, and become another man's, shall he return unto her again? ...thou hast polluted the land with thy whoredoms and with thy wickedness. Therefore the showers have been withholden, and there hath been no latter rain; and thou hadst a whore's forehead, thou refusedst to be ashamed. Wilt thou not from this time cry unto me, My father, thou art the guide of my youth?...And I said after ~~she~~[6213]ashh(accomplish) had done all these things, Turn thou unto me. But ~~she~~[7725]shwvb(return) returned not. And ~~her~~(there is no word here) treacherous ~~sister~~[269]achwvt(other) Judah saw it. And I saw, when for all the causes whereby backsliding Israel committed adultery ~~I had put her away~~[7971]shlch(to send), and given ~~her~~[853]at(a) a bill of divorce;.. yet ~~her~~(there is no word here) treacherous ~~sister~~[269]achwvt(other) Judah feared not, but went and played the harlot also...Go and proclaim these words toward the north, and say, Return, thou backsliding Israel, saith the Lord; and I will not cause mine anger to fall upon you: for I am merciful, saith the Lord, and I will not keep anger for ever. Only acknowledge thine iniquity, that thou hast transgressed against the Lord thy God, and hast scattered thy ways to the strangers under every green tree, and ye have not obeyed my voice, saith the Lord...And I will give you pastors according to mine heart, which shall feed you with knowledge and understanding...In those days the house of Judah shall walk with the house of Israel, and they shall come together out of the land of the north to the land that I have given for an inheritance unto your fathers...We lie down in our shame, and our confusion covereth us: for we have sinned against the Lord our God, we and our fathers, from our youth even unto this day, and have not obeyed the voice of the Lord our God."

Strong's Hebrew 251 'ach'; alike, another, 'each to other', kinship, (can also mean) brother.
Strong's Hebrew 269 'achwvt'; other, another, beloved, (can also mean) sister.

Okay to start with as you can see there is no female being blamed here. Just another example of why I am writing this book. Men, sort yourselves out. Who gave you license to put 'she', 'sister', 'I had put her away', up in that scripture. What a load of tinkering. Mix this folly in Jeremiah with the folly clearly stated in Malachi and we see what needs solving in order for Jesus to come back. Men, get off of that humongous ego, and start Joining with the woman God tells you to Join.

Also note that Israel and Judah now reside in a land of the north; now refer to Rahm Emanuel's proclamation in Chicago mentioned earlier.

It's time for Him to join to us again and Jesus is selecting His ceremonial attire. Now that good thing without spot or wrinkle is His bride; which is a feminine article.

Chapter 3

Truth

I cannot speak for all versions of the bible, as I gave up reading those when I was a child. I once owned a version of the bible which contained most of the books which reportedly have been edited out. After some months of reading it, I found myself praying for dead people that I did not know. Needless to say, after a few months it was consigned to the bin.

Find yourself a bible that you can write your notes in and cross reference with the original Hebrew and Greek texts. Some of the Strong's resources do not use the original text and so assume the bible is repeating the same word just because their bible translation of that word is repeated. Having said that, the original version and all those printed up until Israel was declared a nation again in the 1940s were a good deal more accurate. Edits have been made to some Hebrew texts and therefore some English translations of the Old Testament. The language 'experts' have added vowels to Hebrew words that were never there. They have taken Hebrew letters from the beginning and the end of words and in so doing have made many different words look like the one word. And, they have given words possessing only one meaning, a handful of them.

Had there been significant intelligent deletion of text from the KJV bible, the first thing which would have been removed is Genesis 3:16 where God does not give Eve a curse, quickly followed by Daniel 7:9 and Revelation 1:14-15. In Daniel 7:9 Jesus' hair is described as being like wool (an afro) and Daniel 10:6 says that His body is the colour of polished bronze. Revelation 1:15 says that His feet are like fine brass…burned in a furnace. Some 'bible experts' maintain the wool pertains not to the texture of his hair but to the colour. Firstly, Jesus is not an old man, His hair is not grey. He cannot succumb to old age and infirmity and even if He could it would have to be before He died and was resurrected with a new perfect body. Secondly, the reference in Daniel 7:9 tells us He is sitting down and His hair is like pure wool, not the white colour of wool that some sheep have (not all sheep have white wool). In Revelation 1:15 He is standing up, fully glorified with what some call His 'third eye'/'brow and crown chakras' illuminated. So His hair is glowing. The colour of his hair still being that of any young man's 'fro.

That said, there are a good few discrepancies in bible commentaries and dictionaries. In mine there is a glaring one in the translation of the word 'Adam'. In Genesis the word 'Adam' is given the Strong's dictionary/concordance number 120, and given the definition; 'from 119 ruddy, i.e. a human being, male, mankind, a masculine noun meaning a male, any human being, or generically the human race. The word is used to signify a man as oppose to a woman...' The preceding entry mentioned here is 119 defined as; 'to show blood in the face, i.e. flush or turn rosy, a verb meaning to be red, ruddy, dyed red.'
So here we are led to believe that God created Adam as red, that Adam does not pertain to women, and that mankind does not consist of women. God clearly says that He created 'adam; male and female (Genesis 1:27). As a result of the fall in Eden we all must address a curse in order to be free. For us ladies, if we want liberty we need to hear directly from God ourselves. More about that later.

If you check the Hebrew Aleph Bet illustrated at the beginning of this book, you can see what each letter means and then amalgamate these meanings and actually discover what God is saying. Adam is spelt Aleph, Dalet, Mem which means 'The first strong door into life', which pertains to melanin, of chemical construct like chlorophyll which is in the same family as dark matter (or anti-matter), the combination of all colours/frequencies, which our universe is made from. However, red is Strong's number 2447 which is 'chklyl'. Genesis 49:12 speaks of eyes being;
"red with wine".
We know that eyes become streaked with a reddish colour when an individual is drunk. Red in Hebrew is spelt Chet, Kaf, Lamed, Yood, Lamed this is a completely different word which means 'The separation of the covering of authority that makes authority.' This is the lack of melanin in the skin which causes difficulties when exposed to the sun.

Proverbs 23:29-31
"Who hath woe? who hath sorrow? who hath contentions? who hath babbling? who hath wounds without cause? who hath redness[2448] of eyes? They that tarry long at the wine; they that go to

seek mixed wine. Look not thou upon the wine when it is red[119], when it giveth his colour in the cup, it moveth itself aright."

119 here is an example of 'experts' tampering with bible study helps. Two errors here. The Strong's says just 'adam', whereas the original Hebrew scriptures say 'ytadm'. Ytadm means 'Making the sign of the first strong door into life'; Yood, Tav, Aleph, Dalet, Mem. Sort of being adam; 'it is brown', earthy or of brownness. Alcohol gets more potent and turns an earthy brown colour when it is mixed; not red. In Strong's, redness 2448 is the Hebrew word 'chkllwvt' and means 'The separation of the covering of authority; authority is securely separated.' Very similar to chklyl above. 2448 and 119 have nothing whatsoever in common with each other. Why you may well ask have they been translated as redness and red. You are now on the right track. The fast track to the Creator.

So, we should read;

"Who hath woe? who hath sorrow? who hath contentions? who hath babbling? who hath wounds without cause? who hath redness[2448] of eyes? They that tarry long at the wine; they that go to seek mixed wine. Look not thou upon the wine when it is earthy[119], when it giveth his colour in the cup, it moveth itself aright."

We are further led to believe in Exodus 25:4-5

"And blue and purple, and scarlet, and fine linen, and goats' And rams' skins dyed red, and badgers' skins, and shittim wood,…"

that the words 'dyed red" are correctly translated from the word 'adm' ('meaddamim' in some older Hebrew texts). The word 'dyed' is Strong's word 2556 found in Isaiah 63:1, "Who is this that cometh from Edom, with dyed garments from Bozrah?..." In Hebrew 'chmtz' means 'dyed'. So what the bible actually says is;

"And blue and purple, and scarlet, and fine linen, and goats' And rams' skins brown, and badgers' skins, and shittim wood,…"

We can clearly see 'adm' in both 'adm' and 'meaddamim', but there is no 'chamets/hamas' in the word adam. So Exodus 25:5 does not say 'dyed red'. It is another attempt to try to make the first created adam a red male who has nothing to do with women. In changing the meaning of adam for the purposes of formulating this Caucasian/Aryan male precedent, the lie must be further perpetuated throughout the scriptures by reason of the fact that the translation of 'adm' must always then become 'red'. Adam; Aleph, Dalet, Mem; The first strong door into life, Earth/soil. As mentioned before, adm is a verb, which denotes that it is a 'doing word'. It is not an adjective and it is not a noun. The Strong's says it is a verb; 'A verb meaning to be red, ruddy, dyed red.' So why in the hell the Strong's goes ahead and overlaps itself with connotations referring to adjectives and nouns, I just do not know. A verb gives an action, an occurrence or a state of being. So what is the state of being 'red'? A verb is not a colour. Adm is not red. Adm/Adam is the denotation of a state; a state of being created from the earth as the first strong door into life on this planet.

Additional definitions in this Strong's concordance for adam 120 are: '…another, hypocrite, common sort, low, man (mean, of low degree), person.' Err.. okay. I thought God said He made them perfect. Who are you talking about now mr expert linguist/historian?

Perhaps they want to divert our attention from this woeful fallen state of man, of which we are partaker, and engage our gaze up to the fraudster in the confessional booth, and give him some money… okay, here's ten percent…

So when you read the bible and some bits are not making linear sense, like Adam and Eve being Caucasian when we know the earliest civilizations were on the Asiatic continents (way, way pre-colonialism), you need to get all grown up and go ahead and study it out in Hebrew/Greek.

There is a warning given through John in the book of Revelation which says there are consequences for anyone who takes anything away from that book, to be found in Revelation 22:19. Apart from that, every other book written in the bible was written after it had happened. There are some books containing prophecy for the end of the world as we know it, but these are written amongst other contexts. Thus far, I have not noticed any discrepancies in the book of Revelation.

The Old Testament does not contain an exhaustive list of Hebrew words. Many bible 'scholars' feel the need to make one word spelt with the same Hebrew letters mean a number of different things. There are many entries in the Strong's concordance for the three letters Aleph, Dalet, Mem. In each entry, the Hebrew letters stay the same and erroneous vowels are added which are not in the original Hebrew Scriptures. They also omit important letters from words which *do* make them different. These additions and omissions are like food additives and processing. If you want to eat an apple, the best way to do so is to pick it fresh from an organic tree. An apple flavour chewy bar is not the same thing.

So, what I am I saying here? Study to show thyself approved (2 Timothy 2:15). Sisters, we need to wake up and smell the coffee. Most of the interpretation, sermons and beliefs about the bible/women are idle, scripturally unfounded and written by fake experts. And to my brothers, stop perpetuating the nonsense. The smell of coffee has been attempting to wake us all up for a while and has now stopped percolating.
We need to wake up and smell the coffin. Ill-advised fraudsters are attempting to describe to you your God and the content of the book that is in your own hands. Read and study it for yourself. You do not need anybody to teach you once you have understood the basics of salvation (1 John 2:27, John 8:36). The term 'bible commentary' is an oxymoron.

It's like your uncle is inviting you to stay with him for a month in Naples, Italy. He can show you around for the first week but he owns a big corporation and will be busy most of the time. So he will lend you his car and introduce you to some of his friends. Do you a) refuse his help, stay with a neighbour and take out your Baedeker/Trip Adviser to move around on foot, communicating via gesticulations, or b) make yourself at home in your uncle's mansion, drive his car, go places with his friends and try to learn the language yourself? No brainer.

What I am doing here is showing you that you can get all the juice out of the bible by correctly translating the words and finding out what God is actually, really saying yourself. No man in a pulpit can analyse your history and biological systems, spirit, needs hopes and dreams and then tell you what is going to taste Good to you, and simultaneously to the whole mismatched congregation;
"O taste and see that the LORD good: blessed the man[1397] trusteth in him." (Psalm 34:8)
you need to do it yourself, for yourself.

By the way, the 1397 definition of the word 'man' above is from the 1396 definition; 'a primitive root; to be strong; ... to prevail, act insolently, exceed,... be great,... be valiant'. Both 1396 and 1397 have exactly the same letters; Gimel, Bet, Reysh, but have silly vowel additions to make us think we are looking at a two different words. They are the same. The entry in Psalms 34:8 for 'man' has the Strong's number 1397, which is defined as follows; 'geber – from 1396, properly a valiant man or warrior, generally a person simply, every one, man, mighty. A masculine noun meaning man...it is used of man but often contains more than just a reference to gender by referring to the nature of a man, usually with overtones of spiritual strength... the word is used to contrast men with women and children...' Oh come on now mr expert, stop with the tom foolery and make up your mind.

The potential of the bible in your hands is that of a living book, attempting to speak the truth to you that will make you free of all lies. You read it + you understand it = total freedom.

Chapter 4

Women A

In Genesis we are told God created. The word 'God' here is Elohim 430, which is a plural word. It comes from the Hebrew feminine singular noun root word 'alah' 422, comprising of the Hebrew letters Aleph, Lamed, Hey, meaning 'The strong leader is revealed', (like the sun in the sky) and in Strong's definition; 'A verb meaning… to put under oath… alah is used to prove someone's guilt or innocence.' The word Elohim is made up of the Hebrew letters: Aleph, Lamed, Hey, Yood , Mem. Therefore Elohim means 'The leading authority reveals what is made from chaos'. Sounds a bit like quantum physics.

Speaking of God's high science, it's like the people who say the story of the Garden of Eden is just that, an allegorical story that we can learn *something* from. Those are foolish people talking foolishness. Before the aeroplane was invented, people looked at the small golden Quimbaya figures made by the Olmec in Columbia and said they were sculptures of bees. Now thousands of years later, every single aeroplane in the sky looks exactly like them. So, may I suggest that God taking woman from man's side is identical to the scientific method now called cloning? Except that God did a far, far superior job because He was using the raw materials that He made in the first place. God said;
"Let Us make man in Our image" Genesis 1:26.
The concept of the plurality of God is termed the Hashalush Hakadosh in Hebrew belief. So, Team God made man 120. We are told in Genesis 1:27;
"So God created man[120] in his own image, in the image of God[430] created he them[853]; male[7145] and female[5347] created he them[853]."
According to God man is both male and female; in the same way that He is. We should not listen to the statements of misinformation given in these concordances and study tools regarding the meaning of the word man 120; 'the word is used to signify a man, as opposed to a woman'.
What a load of nonsense.
The word should never have been translated as man. It does not have the same meaning. Use of the word 'person', 'self', 'being', or even 'one' would be much truer to origin. What a lot of confusion this has caused women. These individuals mean us, our future generations and this

planet in general harm. Like the man who tells you the all time best invention is gunpowder…

God made men and women an equal singular team; operation replenish. We, both men and women need to move away from all dastardly agents and agenda and move towards the Plan of our Creator.

God 430 means 'The leading authority reveals what is made from chaos'. Man 120 (adm) means 'The first strong door into life'. Them 853 is Aleph, Tav, Mem (atm) and means 'particle/atom'. So when God calls 'adam' (men and women) 'them', the 'they' becomes a singular noun; they are of one atom. Male 7145 is 'zkr' and has the Hebrew letters Zayin, Kaf, Reysh; To carve out and allow a person, defined as, 'to be marked and recognised/remembered'. Female 5347 is 'wvnqbh' meaning 'To puncture and reveal', in Hebrew comprising of the letters Wav, Noon, Qoof, bet, Hey; The hook of life is revealed last from inside.

Woman, you are the hook of life revealed last from the inside. You are twice refined by God for a purpose. So let us get out from under our predicament and in so doing, get our men out from under theirs. Remember, woman did not incur a curse in Eden. The result for her was pain in all things to do with bearing children and a desire towards her husband with him 'lording' it over her. Easy to get over that, just put your desire on God and listen to what He says, problem solved.
That in turn gives the room for man to get up from under the curse he is beneath.

In Eden, the snake was cursed; curse is Strong's Greek number 779 'arwvr' Aleph, Reysh, Wav, Reysh; The highest is the first and He is secured as the first. Adam received his curse; (unsatisfactorily also denoted as 779) 'arwvrh'; The highest is the first and he is secured as the first and this is revealed. Meaning God now looks like He is far superior to you, but only because you have fallen so low. Adam's curse was toil in working a hostile earth containing hostile creations.
Men should cleave to their wives all the days of their lives, then God grants them favour. Adam would have received some form of favour and not a curse in Eden, had he cleaved to his woman instead of shunning and blaming her. After all, he was standing right next to her when she was in discussion with the serpent regarding the information that he had given her. Husband cleaving to wife removes the curse; predatory life-forms, toil and death. All of these simply bite the dust

when she shuts out noise and listens to God, with him cleaving to her. Back to Eden. Floetry.

But we are currently living in a profane earth which needs to return back to God. The meaning we have attached to the word 'profanity' in the bible is incorrect. Our understanding of profanity is to utter a four-letter word, 'curse' or 'swear'. In adding these connotations to the word, we entirely miss the point. Jesus let a few choice words leave His mouth when He was dealing with profane people. Jesus' words were not profane, those people were profane. Job caused himself to become irritated by his 'friends' and spoke about his wife grinding with another man. Job was not profane, his 'friends' and circumstances were. God Himself re-iterated a statement that He was making and told Israel that if a man could urinate up a wall then he was fit to go to war. Except God didn't say urinate. Obviously, God cannot be profane, everything that exists tending towards life is created that way by Him. The existence of fallen things is always due to those creations falling of their own free will which He lovingly provides us with in not wanting us to be robots with A.I. So let's stop being high and mighty, super spiritual, full of foolishness, useless people. If we are made in His image, then let us start acting like Him. The God we are with is a cool dude.
It is time to get angry with profane situations. Go ahead and let a few choice four-letter words leave your mouth as you consider the evils in this world, then solve them.

Leviticus 18:21;
"And thou shalt not let any of thy seed pass through the fire to Molech, neither shalt thou profane[2490] the name of thy God: I am the Lord."
2490 in the Strong's Hebrew is 'chll', 'to wound' Chet, Lamed, Lamed; To separate and be led by being led. This word 'chll' has a very similar meaning to the word 'bbl' (babel) Bet, Bet, Lamed; In the house is just in the house and being led by that. Both chll and bbl are like a pointless effort to do essentially nothing of any lasting worth. Like a dog chasing his tail, round and around he goes. So, 'chll' means to wound God by following after a dumb essence.
In the scripture above, God tells Moses how to instruct Israel. It is interesting to note that people were beginning to copy other nations who threw their own children into flames for an offering to dumb gods. Horrendous. As mentioned earlier, please do not get up on a high horse and judge God when He had to get rid of those woeful nations kit and

caboodle. That is the reason why 'the earth was without form and void'. When nations begin to sacrifice their children, it is all over and the number is up for everybody, cue washing cycle. On that subject, what on earth was that big representation of a baby with the severed head doing at the 2012 Olympic ceremony. And why did it get separated into pieces at the end of that presentation.

So, 'profanity' means to wound God. Curse is to fall from God, and to swear, Leviticus 19:12;

"And ye shall not swear[7650] by my name falsely, neither shalt thou profane the name of thy God: I am the Lord."

7650 is 'tshbuwv', 'being under a vow'. Which is Tav, Sheen, Bet, Ayin, Wav; Making the sign of the teeth inside that see; hooked by it. So all in all, nothing like we have been taught that these words in the bible mean. When in a court of law we are told to swear on a bible. That is anathema. James 5:12 tells us to do no such thing;

"But above all things, my brethren, swear not, neither by heaven, neither by the earth, neither by any other oath: but let your yea be yea; and your nay, nay; lest ye fall into condemnation."

So do not. It is not Godly to so swear. That is not a practise of a civilised hearing.

Jesus is the civilising entity. Since He arrived on the planet bad has never been able to prevail completely in anything, and our adversary is defeated. Yet, we have not entered into the victory He afforded us with His blood. Jesus said that after He left and went to His Father and our Father, we would do greater things. Ladies and gentlemen, roll up your sleeves greater things are about to be done by us.

Deuteronomy 24:1-4;

"When a man hath taken a wife, and married her, and it come to pass that she find no favour in his eyes, because he hath found some uncleanness in her: then let him write her a bill of divorcement, and give it in her hand, and send her out of his house. And when she is departed out of his house, she may go and be another man's wife. And if the latter husband hate her, and write her a bill of divorcement, and giveth it in her hand, and sendeth her out of his house; or if the latter husband die, which took her to be his wife; her former husband, which sent her away, may not take her again to be his wife, after that she is defiled; for that is abomination before the Lord: and thou shalt not cause the

land to sin, which the Lord thy God giveth thee for an inheritance."

Matthew 5:31,32;
"It hath been said, Whosoever shall put away his wife, let him give her a writing of divorcement: but I say unto you, That whosoever shall put away his wife, saving for the cause of fornication, causeth her to commit adultery: and whosoever shall marry her that is divorced committeth adultery."

Luke 16:16-18;
"The law and the prophets were until John: since that time the kingdom of God is preached, and every man presseth into it. And it is easier for heaven and earth to pass, than one tittle of the law to fail. Whosoever putteth away his wife, and marrieth another, committeth adultery: and whosoever marrieth her that is put away from her husband committeth adultery."

Mark 10:2-12;
"And the Pharisees came to him, and asked him, Is it lawful for a man to put away his wife? tempting him. And he answered and said unto them, What did Moses command you? And they said, Moses suffered to write a bill of divorcement, and to put her away. And Jesus answered and said unto them, For the hardness of your heart he wrote you this precept. But from the beginning of the creation God made them male and female. For this cause shall a man leave his father and mother, and cleave to his wife; and they twain shall be one flesh: so then they are no more twain, but one flesh. What therefore God hath joined together, let not man put asunder. And in the house his disciples asked him again of the same matter. And he saith unto them, Whosoever shall put away his wife, and marry another, committeth adultery against her. And if a woman shall put away her husband, and be married to another, she committeth adultery."

N.B. " 'For the hardness of your heart he wrote you this precept.' " Jesus said that about God. The whole bible essentially is written to men in an attempt by God to ameliorate for their hardness of hearts. All of those laws and precepts – hard heart guys. None of the authors in the bible are women. The part of the bible written concerning the affairs of women was written by Paul, who openly admits that he is not an expert on the subject. So, let me suggest to all women that you go to the throne room your own self and get some hot freshly baked biscuits from God, made just the way you like them.

I hope these scriptures make more sense now. All those things God says are to try to restructure man that has no clue, and woman that is still busy listening to the man instead of God.
If God Joined the two of you stay together. If God didn't Join the two of you, He doesn't see you as one. You cannot invite God to the picnic after you have eaten the fried chicken. He is not a vagabond. He will not even recognise your Join, and in addition we see in Malachi that each negative Join can have far reaching adverse connotations for the whole planet. That means it can have a knock on effect that destabilizes all of our futures.

A man can marry anybody, but he only has one wife. God actually delineates the two words; married is Strong's number 1166, 'bal', yep baal. As in Bet, Ayin, Lamed; 'The household experiences control'. Wife is 'asht', Aleph, Sheen, Tav; 'The first devouring sign', which denotes victory over the mistakes of Eden.
God will sanctify your children if you have just taken up with whomever you choose, no matter who you are. However, you two are not one in His eyes if He did not agree to your Joining together. If as a believer you are dictating who you are going to Join with and not seeking His guidance, then you are being god to your own self in the biggest decision you make on earth outside knowing your Creator. Choosing your own spouse without involving God is like deciding to get born again, but as an apple.
So in view of those facts, the scriptures above make complete fair sense. They are not the ramblings of a cranky God. We are trying to move the whole planet forward here with the principle 'atoms' male and female. As we read in Hebrews 1:12, there will be a time when the earth is folded up like a garment and all this law and marriage disappear. Are we there yet? No.

However, we believers are dead to the law, Romans 7:1-6;
"Know ye not, brethren, (for I speak to them that know the law,) how that the law hath dominion over a man as long as he liveth? For the woman which hath an husband is bound by the law to her husband so long as he liveth; but if the husband be dead, she is loosed from the law of her husband. So then if, while her husband

84

liveth, she be married to another man, she shall be called an adulteress: but if her husband be dead, she is free from that law; so that she is no adulteress, though she be married to another man. Wherefore, my brethren, ye also are become dead to the law by the body of Christ; that ye should be married to another, even to him who is raised from the dead, that we should bring forth fruit unto God. For when we were in the flesh, the motions of sins, which were by the law, did work in our members to bring forth fruit unto death. But now we are delivered from the law, that being dead wherein we were held; that we should serve in newness of spirit, and not in the oldness of the letter."

The mysteries of God and the destiny of this planet are tied up in this thing called Joining Together. It is obvious. It was the garden of Eden and two Joined people that messed up. So Joined people have been given the anointing to put it right, as Malachi says in the last book before the gospels. The correction needed is now on a global scale to be delivered by His believers, touting His Opinion = the Glory of God.

God told me it rains on everybody. I asked Him why evil men prosper. He said because they catch blessings. I said why are they able to catch the rain. He said because it's raining.

We have to learn how to put our righteous believing buckets out there. Sometimes you have to put yourself in strange positions that do not seem 'holy' in order to catch the rain, refresh yourself and others and continue in strength. But you know what, holy just means being set apart for God. Nothing else. Look at Hosea, he was told to Join himself with a prostitute. God told him to do that because God wanted to show all of us wisdom. Then look at Mary who washed Jesus' feet with her hair, and was at that point a prostitute. The same Mary who was sister to Lazurus at the home Jesus loved best to chill in. Jesus was not sleeping with her as some illiterate idiots suggest. Can they read? The fact is that He enjoyed their company; Martha, Mary and Lazarus because they were real people trying to get on in a really fallen world. They were honest people that He could relate to. That is why some of the pious people of the time said He ate too much and drank too much. He was enjoying Himself with down to earth people because He was a real man who liked real people.

So, when we look at the 99% ers and wonder when God will judge them and stop letting them get rich on 99% of the earth's wealth whilst 99.99: % of the earth's population live on 1% of the wealth, we need to stop a minute. Get yourself in the right position, get the biggest bucket ever conceived and catch you some serious rain. If God tells you to take up an awkward position, all the better. Awkward is the wisdom of God. It means your life is about to take off in the heavens, it is for a sign, a song to God, and good people around you will believe and change for the better, like Mary did.

We are all dead to the law because we are alive in Christ. My God, we need to wake up and make a move. What is the first new move we need to make? Men love your wives. Which means women, be beautiful. Woman, it is your duty to be beautiful. Men it is your beauty to be dutiful. That could be the whole book right there. That is the Ephesians 6:14-18 Armour of God.

There are two ingredients to manhood: 1) love woman 2) say what you mean and mean what you say. That is it. Voila you have the perfect man. Any woman who meets him and falls in love with him for real will stay with him for ever. The premise of manhood is such an easy one. It is beautiful in its simplicity. That is why we women love men.

The definition of real beauty that does not fade and is not vain is in the book of Proverbs chapter 31:10-31;

"Who can find a virtuous woman? for her price is far above rubies. The heart of her husband doth safely trust in her, so that he shall have no need of spoil. She will do him good and not evil all the days of her life. She seeketh wool, and flax, and worketh willingly with her hands. She is like the merchants' ships; she bringeth her food from afar. She riseth also while it is yet night, and giveth meat to her household, and a portion to her maidens. She considereth a field, and buyeth it: with the fruit of her hands she planteth a vineyard. She girdeth her loins with strength, and strengtheneth her arms. She perceiveth that her merchandise is good: her candle goeth not out by night. She layeth her hands to the spindle, and her hands hold the distaff. She stretcheth out her hand to the poor; yea, she reacheth forth her hands to the needy. She is not afraid of the snow for her household: for all her household are clothed with scarlet. She maketh herself coverings of tapestry; her clothing is silk and purple. Her husband is known in the gates, when he sitteth among the elders of the land. She maketh fine linen, and selleth it; and delivereth girdles unto the merchant. Strength and

honour are her clothing; and she shall rejoice in time to come. She openeth her mouth with wisdom; and in her tongue is the law of kindness. She looketh well to the ways of her household, and eateth not the bread of idleness. Her children arise up, and call her blessed; her husband also, and he praiseth her. Many daughters have done virtuously, but thou excellest them all. Favour is deceitful, and beauty is vain: but a woman that feareth the Lord, she shall be praised. Give her of the fruit of her hands; and let her own works praise her in the gates."

Many believing women find the Proverbs 31 woman a daunting shoe to try to squeeze into. Let me simplify it for you. Stop shopping and start selecting things wisely. That will cover it and you will speedily grow into her through your own personal touch of charisma. Girls shop. Women go to market and trade with one another.

When we get together with our minds made up we do astounding things, Matthew 28:1-10;
"In the end of the sabbath, as it began to dawn toward the first day of the week, came Mary Magdalene and the other Mary to see the sepulchre. And, behold, there was a great earthquake: for the angel of the Lord descended from heaven, and came and rolled back the stone from the door, and sat upon it. His countenance was like lightning, and his raiment white as snow: And for fear of him the keepers did shake, and became as dead men. And the angel answered and said unto the women, Fear not ye: for I know that ye seek Jesus, which was crucified. He is not here: for he is risen, as he said. Come, see the place where the Lord lay. And go quickly, and tell his disciples that he is risen from the dead; and, behold, he goeth before you into Galilee; there shall ye see him: lo, I have told you. And they departed quickly from the sepulchre with fear and great joy; and did run to bring his disciples word. And as they went to tell his disciples, behold, Jesus met them, saying, All hail. And they came and held him by the feet, and worshipped him. Then said Jesus unto them, Be not afraid: go tell my brethren that they go into Galilee, and there shall they see me."

Bless that guy Jesus, don't you just love Him? He is sooo beautiful.

Meanwhile, our men are still chasing their tails, John 20:1-9;

"The first day of the week cometh Mary Magdalene early, when it was yet dark, unto the sepulchre, and seeth the stone taken away from the sepulchre. Then she runneth, and cometh to Simon Peter, and to the other disciple, whom Jesus loved, and saith unto them, ~~They have taken away~~[142]eran(raise) the Lord out of the sepulchre, and we know not where ~~they have laid~~[5087]ethecan(established) him. Peter therefore went forth, and that other disciple, and came to the sepulchre. So they ran both together: and the other disciple did outrun Peter, and came first to the sepulchre. And he stooping down, and looking in, saw the linen clothes lying; yet went he not in. Then cometh Simon Peter following him, and went into the sepulchre, and seeth the linen clothes lie, And the napkin, that was about his head, not lying with the linen clothes, but wrapped together in a place by itself. Then went in also that other disciple, which came first to the sepulchre, and he saw, and believed. For as yet they knew not the scripture, that he must rise again from the dead."

All that falsified information written by the confounded, completely wrongly translating the bible for the benefit of themselves. Mary didn't come in all blonde and dizzy saying 'they have taken Him'. She said He was raised. She didn't say she did not know where 'they have laid' Him, she said she didn't know where He then established Himself. A whole heap of difference. She knew exactly what had happened and why He was not in the tomb anymore.

It seems that the women somehow knew that Jesus was going to resurrect. Maybe it is something to do with the fact that they heard it from the grapevine Himself, instead of waiting for a man to give them his own watered down version of the truth. She was so unbelievably happy that in running so fast to deliver the news she left Jesus' mother behind.

Buckle up ladies, there is work to be done.

Look what Paul reported, 1 Corinthians 15:4-8;
"And that he was buried, and that he rose again the third day according to the scriptures: And that he was seen of Cephas, then of the twelve: After that, he was seen of above five hundred brethren at once; of whom the greater part remain unto this present, but some are fallen asleep. After that, he was seen of

James; then of all the apostles. And last of all he was seen of me also, as of one born out of due time."

Err, Paul, what about the sisters?..Like I say sisters, the bible is an awesome book. Please read it as if God has something to say to you, specifically you; as the twice refined. Paul did not mention us women, but check this out, as we know that all scripture is given, 2 Timothy 3:16, 17;
"…by inspiration of God, and is profitable for doctrine, for reproof, for correction, for instruction in righteousness: That the man[444] of God may be perfect, thoroughly furnished unto all good works."
444 is 'anthropos', like anthropology and means people. Therefore read 'people of God'.

Mark 16:6,7;
"And he saith unto them, Be not affrighted: Ye seek Jesus of Nazareth, which was crucified: he is risen; he is not here: behold the place where they laid him. But go your way, tell his disciples and Peter that he goeth before you into Galilee: there shall ye see him, as he said unto you."
The angel tells Mary Magdalene, Mary and Salome to tell the disciples and Peter, inferring that Peter at that point was not a disciple. Now look at Luke 8:1-3 and Mark 15:39-41;
"And it came to pass afterward, that he went throughout every city and village, preaching and shewing the glad tidings of the kingdom of God: and the twelve were with him, And certain women, which had been healed of evil spirits and infirmities, Mary called Magdalene, out of whom went seven devils, And Joanna the wife of Chuza Herod's steward, and Susanna, and many others, which ministered unto him of their substance."

"And when the centurion, which stood over against him, saw that he so cried out, and gave up the ghost, he said, Truly this man was the Son of God. There were also women looking on afar off: among whom was Mary Magdalene, and Mary the mother of James the less and of Joses, and Salome; (Who also, when he was in Galilee, followed him, and ministered unto him;) and many other women which came up with him unto Jerusalem."

The bible never once calls any of the women that followed Jesus 'disciples'. Actually because they were not.

In those times, and in modern judicial history up until a few decades ago, men were the only gender deemed fit to give legally binding testimony. Therefore God would obviously need to choose men to offer this testimony for such a crucial case. It is the premise of God and Judaism that formulates our world today. 12 clans of Israel, 12 disciples, 12 people on a jury. God goes with the flow of what is currently going on with His man in order to get His message across to us. That does not mean it is His preferred way of doing things. We see this in the divorce scriptures mentioned where He says that the law was put in place because of the hardness of heart in males. We can throw that reasoning over the whole of the all laws written by God for people in the Old Testament; hardness of heart being the qualifier for their existence, or else Adam would have been far more generous to Eve in his response to God regarding wilfully chewing and swallowing a mouthful of apple. Nobody forced him to eat at gunpoint and he was the one who personally received the instruction from God vis a vis not to.

The word disciple is 'limud' in Hebrew meaning 'taught' and 'mathétés' in Greek meaning a learner/pupil. Everything that the disciples did of lasting value before Jesus died was something that they needed to be taught how to accomplish by Jesus. The women with Jesus supported Him with their finances. Jesus did not walk up to certain females who looked rich and instruct them to hand over some cash. These women did it because they innately knew that it needed to be done. These many other women who were with Him throughout His ministry and remained at the foot of the cross until they were moved further back by the soldiers as He died were the supporting force that enabled the ministry to be. They operated with all of their substance, by organising things. Again we see a misnomer, they were not all ex-demon possessed. Among the women in the cohort was Jesus' mother, so we can put that idea in the bin straight off.

So, what are we as women? We are organic beings who compute, register and install secure futures for our men to walk in. We engineer paths sometimes with our wombs, sometimes with our hands and sometimes with our substance like the proverbs 31 woman.

Men, you should now be brethren of Jesus, Matthew 28:10. Brothers are not all the same. They share family characteristics but are still unique. They flow in the physical charisma of the family and have no need to be taught how to be a brother. Jesus never calls the women 'sisters' because after He died, their hook up remains a feasibility exercise in hearing and doing what is missing. Same way she was created in Eden. Nothing has changed. The only difference is that now Jesus has left His Holy Spirit we have the get go to grow and then to become moulded as one with that Holy Spirit. The Holy Spirit is called the 'helper'. That is the same as we women uneqebah; 'The hook of life is revealed last from inside', so we can flow together with our men, bounce off this planet and move.

So the pattern is; we make disciples of all nations. After having received the teaching, men become brothers in Him and women become uneqebah; unique instruments of God Almighty in their own situations.

Women need to cut loose from the madness and be women. And that is all. The fear of the Lord is the beginning of wisdom, not the fear of a man. So for the woman, asking God directly what's up is all she needs to do, otherwise she will be living more or less as fallen; cleaving to the man and having him lord it over her. For the man's sake, he must hear god AND get wisdom. In the garden of Eden the male heard God yet watched powerlessly whilst his woman got up to all kind of foolishness based upon the fact that she trusted her man's apoplexy and didn't go direct to God for her information. She tried to use her 'wiles' to work out what the shape of things were and what therefore was going on. No. Sister, that is not it. Yes we know we as the feminine part can perceive things and we have a gifted sense of knowing, but God Knows. He has a mouth and He is always talking. He is in the business of talking. That is how He creates and that is how He created you; to be a speaking creating spirit. In being a beautiful speaking creating spirit you will always naturally be in line with the bible.

Women need to feed their men with wisdom, Romans 10:1-3;

"Brethren, my heart's desire and prayer to God for Israel is, that they might be saved. For I bear them record that they have a zeal of God, but not according to knowledge. For they being ignorant of God's righteousness, and going about to establish their own righteousness, have not submitted themselves unto the righteousness of God."

We love your zeal guys but you need to hold it down in favour of knowledge. Let us hold good men up with wisdom and replenish the earth together, taking it back to its former glory, Proverbs 4:7;

"Wisdom is the principal thing; therefore get wisdom: and with all thy getting get understanding."

In a nutshell, for this dispensation of life anyway. Men need to get wisdom whether by Joining their wife (be sure, there is one and only one out there for him) or by cuddling up to wisdom, cleaving to it and never letting it go, as Paul did. John always made sure Jesus was never far away from him, so that He could influence his own thinking and destiny. John ended up being the only male left standing at the foot of the cross.

If Adam had answered God in wisdom, with love towards his woman in Eden there would have been no need for them to leave. That is why Adam got the curse and Eve just got held back, in spite of the fact that they both ate and Eve initiated. We have to wait for our men to love us properly first before we get to do anything great, just like Paul says.

So, what does this new man look like? He looks like Jesus, he looks like David.

God loves David. When David was provoked to number Israel God did not consider it to be a sin. He was set up by the adversary in the same way that Eve was set up by the adversary to eat from the tree of good and evil. Eve's act resulted in a curse on Adam, and great sorrow for her. David's act resulted in a pestilence on Israel and great sorrow for him. So you see that David is cut from a type of loving cloth. He was a very loving man. His only sin in God's eyes was in the matter with Uriah and his wife Bathsheba. And yet God says David brought joy to Israel and that he was a man after God's own heart.

David was chased from pillar to post from the time he was young to the time he finally took up his seat as the King of Israel. He endured with humility, with wisdom and with honour. All the while knowing he was the true anointed king over Israel.

David had an excuse as to why he did not manage to settle down with one woman. His head was not clear because he lived in pain. He was in a dispensation without the Holy Spirit and so had to rely on his own emotions to regulate his spirit. This is why the Psalms are so deep; he had to write his spirit out. He grew up on the backside of nowhere with a bunch of sheep, defending himself as a small child against lions. His father's wife was not his mother and he was a young outcast from his house. A man who lives like that would have to be Jesus Himself in order not to fall into the arms of the first warm woman that came his way.

David was a lover of women and Bathsheba his last wife bore him sons including, Solomon and Nathan, counted in the genealogy of Joseph and Mary respectively.

Let us assume the average man has not been anointed king of Israel and has not had to defend himself against lions as a child. If he is to be the new improved man, then he is like David a man of his word, he always says what he means and he always means what he says. Secondly, he loves women. That is it and bingo. Simple. As he is not being hotly pursued by lions, we can also assume that he has time to wait for God to tell him who his wife is.

For those women who either fell in with the wrong man or are still waiting for the right one there is good hope, Isaiah 54:1;

"Sing, O barren, thou that didst not bear; break forth into singing, and cry aloud, thou that didst not travail²³⁴² ~~with child~~: for more are the children¹¹²¹ of the desolate⁸⁰⁷⁴ than the children of the married¹¹⁶⁶ wife, saith the Lord."

The Good News keeps coming ladies, we need to subscribe to that paper. 2342 as in many occurrences in the Strong's is a word that is supposed to magically be the same as other words which are clearly spelt differently. The word given under 2342 is 'chwvl', but in the original text it is 'chlh'. Chlh is used only twice in the bible, in the scripture above and in Isaiah 68:8;

"Who hath heard such a thing? who hath seen such things? Shall the earth be made to bring forth in one day? or shall a nation be born at once? for as soon as Zion travailed²³⁴², she brought forth her children."

So we can see that chlh does not just pertain to women. This type of travailing is to 'Fence what the authority has revealed'; Chet, Lamed, Hey and can be performed by a nation for its people.

1121 in Isaiah 54:1 is 'bny', Bet, Noon, Yood; 'In the house life is made', meaning offspring and general ancestry of the family name and quality. 8074 is 'swvmm' which means 'stupified'. 1166 is buwvlh' which means 'mastered over'. So Isaiah 54:1 paraphrased says:

'Sing if nothing has happened in your life yet that you know is your glorious destiny. Shout out your song if it has not happened yet. For more is the greatness that is about to come out of you, who has been totally stupefied by all the madness so far in your life, than all of the 'greatness' you think you have seen from all the 'successful' people in this world system'.

Sounds like another scripture, Isaiah 60:1-5;

"Arise, shine; for thy light is come, and the glory of the Lord is risen upon thee. For, behold, the darkness shall cover the earth, and gross darkness the people: but the Lord shall arise upon thee, and his glory shall be seen upon thee. And the Gentiles shall come to thy light, and kings to the brightness of thy rising. Lift up thine eyes round about, and see: all they gather themselves together, they come to thee: thy sons shall come from far, and thy daughters shall be nursed at thy side. Then thou shalt see, and flow together, and thine heart shall fear, and be enlarged; because the abundance of the sea shall be converted unto thee, the forces of the Gentiles shall come unto thee."

Time to rejoice.

Chapter 5

Women Bee

This chapter is strictly for the ladies. Men reading it may come unstuck. You have been duly warned.

Women are capable of parthenogenesis. That is, to produce offspring without fertilization. I.e., no man in sight. Biologically a woman would only be able to have female children through this process, this is called parthenogenic thelytoky. Arrhenotoky is a form of parthenogenesis whereby in the absence of fertilization, only males can be produced. Deuterotoky is the parthenogenic production of both male and female offspring.
If a group of female bees are in need of a male, they can transmit a frequency which transforms a female drone into a male.

Scientific theory tells us that men have both x and y chromosomes and women have just x. Science becomes real when it indicates itself as true in other disciplines. For example, gravity was known to be a force, but mathematical calculations could not bear that premise, and so now we know gravity is relationship; relativity. If we take the bible as a discipline, we can see that woman came out of man. So the elements of woman are in man. As God did not scrape all the woman-ness out of every part of the man it would be fair to say that there remains in male the driving factor of female which is the creating nurturing force.

We have gone through the process of Eden and the resulting fall in order for men to see that creating side of them and to learn to articulate it. God took Eve out of Adam so he could see what was already inside him, and move in company, confidence and power with her to subdue the earth. That subjugation is still pending because Adam as a whole still cannot see.

When I saw the man I love, I saw a great big gap that I could nestle into, yet still stand shoulder to shoulder with him. His eyes looked like vulnerable city and I knew he could see me inside of him.

The force of our God is His ability to create us as one in an identikit of Himself. Second to that come His omnipotence, omnipresence and omniscience. A portion of omniscience was garnered by Adam and Eve after eating from the tree of knowledge. God removed them from the garden before they could eat of omnipresence via the everlasting life tree. Now, men are not bees. They are not drones and women cannot transform them. As a matter of fact, we do not want our men altered at all. God knows, we love them just as they are. However, In order for men to win, they must undergo the opposite of transformation, which is to unfold who they already are.

Women were much sought after in ancient times by angels. When these angels began to take women for wives, God did not call the offspring that they had evil. In fact He said that these women bore many of the mighty men of old. However, it grieved God's spirit that this process was leaving out His man. But His men were behaving badly, Genesis 6:1-8;

"And it came to pass, when men began to multiply on the face of the earth, and daughters were born unto them, That the sons of God saw the daughters of men that they were fair[2896]**twvb** ('an adjective meaning good, well pleasing, fruitful, morally correct, proper, convenient.')**; and they took them wives of all which they chose. And the Lord said, My spirit shall not always strive with man, for that he also is flesh: yet his days shall be an hundred and twenty years. There were giants in the earth in those days; and also after that, when the sons of God came in unto the daughters of men, and they bare children to them, the same became mighty men which were of old, men of renown. And God saw that the wickedness of man was great in the earth, and that every imagination of the thoughts of his heart was only evil continually. And it repented the Lord that he had made man on the earth, and it grieved him at his heart. And the Lord said, I will destroy man whom I have created from the face of the earth; both man, and beast, and the creeping thing, and the fowls of the air; for it repenteth me that I have made them. But Noah found grace in the eyes of the Lord."**

It would have been another case of rinse and repeat if it hadn't been for Noah. Noah had one wife. Note, Noah had one wife. Note Abraham had, yes you guessed it, one wife. These are the men that God relied on when the whole of His creation was on the line.

Abraham was told that all the promises of God for a holy nation would come through him. Yet, Abraham lived and died without a single crumb of the law. He knew innately the treasure that Sarah was to him.

May I suggest that in order for the Body of Christ to come together women will need to be seen as the glue. Ephesians 4:16;
"From whom the whole body fitly joined together and compacted by that which every joint supplieth, according to the effectual working in the measure of every part, maketh increase of the body unto the edifying of itself in love."

In parts of the African continent it is tradition for children to ask permission and advice from their mother before they do anything for the day. Permission just to get up in the morning. The sons stop asking permission when they Join with their wives. The daughters stop when they Join with their husbands and the tradition continues. You are only Hebrew if your mother is Hebrew which locates the whole faith in a matriarchal context. So why on earth are we dealing still with this hard hearted men business. It is time to stop the clock, come outside into the fresh air and get on with living in the balance that God created.

The operation of both the home and society as a whole need to emanate from one mind. If they do not, we are left with the chaotic picture that we have at the moment where everything is fractured and we are led to believe that all is well in utopia, utopia is all that matters and there really is nobody experiencing calamitous suffering, as we sit and watch some silly tv show, munching some pretend food, having returned from a futile job.
When societies are matriarchal things tick like clockwork without the need for a controlling timepiece. When a household is organised and executed by one mind, that one mind can make dexterously fine adjustments to that household based on correlating computations within one mind. Like the Proverbs 31 woman, she is praised and her husband is a great man, known among other men seated in authority. Like Abraham was, due to his diligence over Sarah, who moved the household along.

Come on ladies, you know you can do all the handyman stuff around the house; if you were given your sweet time to find somebody to teach you and weren't rushed off your feet all the while. You would dearly love to spend what you give the handyman on something a little more interesting. I can tell you, fixing things around the house is something of a doddle when you know how. Everything to do with the home, the children, the market place and local government should be largely the seat of women. The interests of each household being presented at various levels of community, creating real, righteous government structures. Beyond this point is where men come in, which I will deal with in another book. There are permutations, some women being more delicate and unable to do household d.i.y. How do you define delicate? If you are a woman who doesn't mind people seeing you cry, you are delicate. In which case, you are a more ostentatious creature, like a flower, whereas the rest of us women are more like a juicy piece of fruit that cannot be resisted. The flower came first, then the fruit, so feel free to change up whenever, thou delicate woman.

It all fits in with the regimen of the bespoke husband and wife team, never the same; always a differing balance of attributes.

Men have to learn to love completely and effectually; as non birthing creations. This makes them superior to the devil who is, as the angels a non birthing creature. There are no female angels. The only creatures that have both spirit and creative ability are the Godlike creatures. That equals God, women and men. That is why the angels desired to look into the creation of man because they marvelled at the fact and matter.

In Genesis 48:16 'evil' is 'ru' = Reysh, Ayin; The head exposer. So men will need to stop exposing women as Adam did in Eden. In exposing us they are exposing themselves and many boxershorts are showing throughout the land. It is just plain evil and God got tired with it all once, and Noah intervened. Even then He only saved Noah and co. So you need to really actually be in The family of Faith this time in order for God to let your genes continue on to the next dispensation of this planet.

If all were to fail, you know and men never could correct, He could reach in His bag of stuff to create something a little closer to angels, being without a feminine element so that they would jump out o'heaven to get to us ladies. Be warned, it has happened before and the product was men of renown. But it is not what God wants because it is not His best.

Women everywhere pray. Pray continuously. When Paul said that we should pray continuously you know he did not mean praying in an uncomfortable position (like on your knees, what's up with that?), getting up at stupid o'clock to wake the whole house with babbling every morning, or shouting at the top of your voice. Now on the odd occasion you may do these things for want of a better way to communicate with God in order to find your forward button. However you can do none of the above continuously. Continuously means the opposite of all of the above. In continuous mode you are comfy enough to hear His every intonation, you have the hot line to God open at all times. You are always hearing Him. You sleep tonnes of sleep so that you sufficiently and perfectly hear His message to you. You know He gives His beloved sleep, Psalm 127:1,2;

"Except the Lord build the house, they labour in vain that build it: except the Lord keep the city, the watchman waketh but in vain. It is vain for you to rise up early, to sit up late, to eat the bread of sorrows: for so he giveth his beloved sleep."

So go ahead and catch those zzz's. Dreams are a whole nother realm, which would take half a book to explain. Being spiritual is not some old pious crispyness. The word for spirit is pnuema, where we get our words pneumonia or pneumatic drill. Pnuema is to be filled to pressure with air; or filled to power with God's breath. All the time. When you breathe in you breathe in God. You breathe, you walk, you talk to Him. continually. That is where the discipline of yoga comes from. It is not some out there abomination, it was actually a part of our routine when our wise ancestors would meditate with God. Also when people like David pick up a wind instrument and play it, lift up their voice and sing, or dance knowing they are dancing in front of Him and regulating their breathing. It doesn't need to be in a church building, in fact, that is the last place that it is going to be effective. Why people continue to gather every Sunday for the purposes of warming pews and scratching each other's backs I will never fathom. Paul said forsake not the assembling of yourselves together, not the arbitrary gathering. That's like putting a pile of car parts in the road and expecting to drive off inside them to do something of importance.

You can dance before the Lord in any club of your choosing. Just like Jesus, He went to all the base places of His time, turned the people around to righteousness, and went right on chilling in those same establishments. Take it from me, a nobody called donkey rock, I have done it before and it properly works. It will astound you, John 14:12;

"Verily, verily, I say unto you, He that believeth on me, the works that I do shall he do also; and greater works than these shall he do; because I go unto my Father."

We need to start looking at this whole picture differently. Particularly women, we need to start seeing. When a woman has a child she becomes a mother and makes a man a father, this horizon event can be viewed by each woman. It is an open book for any clued up woman to look inside of herself and see how it is that God is knitting her baby together. It is there right inside of her body, another one with a spirit. That womb is power, we women should get together and have womb health and preservation clubs. We should call them maternities.

Do you know that the humble raspberry leaf keeps your womb in good health? Then stupid retches came along and made the East India company and told us all to drink some calcified carcinogenic burnt leaves. Whereas, back in the day women in the know would make tea from raspberry leaves, wood avens and the like in order to stay productive and healthy. Are there any female gynaecologists out there, men so love that job, I wonder why. Ladies, can you step out of the mad machine for a minute and get together to do some real scientific study? Find out if this whole menopause nonsense is supposed to happen to us or whether it is just vitamin/mineral deficiency following 40 years of menstruation. Check out some women on less interrupted continents and see if they have histories of menopausal issues in their lineage. Our menstrual cycle is connected to the cycle of our moon, and hence our knowledge and understanding of the movements on our planet. As a young girl I was bombarded with revelations from the God during menstruation. Now the revelations are a constant flow. When men thought us to be getting out of hand regarding our Godly knowledge they called it Lunar-cy; lunacy. Go figure. We need to make a consolidated move with this information. It is not a man's world; if anything, the opposite, Psalm 145:9;

"The Lord is good to all: and his tender mercies[7356]**rchm**('the womb; as cherishing the foetus') **are over all his works."**

Remember. Ladies, Jesus is of the seed of David through Mary not Joseph, Acts 2:30, Romans 1:3, 2 Samuel 7:12;

"Therefore being a prophet, and knowing that God had sworn with an oath to him, that of the fruit of his loins, according to the flesh, he would raise up Christ to sit on his throne;"

"Concerning his Son Jesus Christ our Lord, which was made of the seed of David according to the flesh;"

"And when thy days be fulfilled, and thou shalt sleep with thy fathers, I will set up thy seed after thee, which shall proceed out of thy bowels, and I will establish his kingdom."

Chapter 6

Therefore

Mary was steadfast in what the angel of the Lord told her, knowing that she could be stoned to death if she kept Jesus in her womb. She knew however that passing through this life is as a nothing compared to responding to a spark from God. So she juxtapositioned herself against the spirit of the world, and leant very heavily on the Spirit of God.

It was no happenstance that God chose Mary's womb. The evidence is her cousin Elisabeth. Elisabeth's womb was also chosen by God for John. Judging by the fact that Elisabeth's husband Zachariah was struck dumb in the synagogue because he would not believe, we can safely say that the sisters received from God because it was they who were in effectual contact with God. They had Him on the hotline. Mary and Elisabeth were as gods on earth, ambassadors for our home country, heaven. They were cousins, so John and Jesus were cousins. God was able to prepare Jesus' path by John, and therefore deliver Jesus to us to save this whole planet because of two female cousins.

Now, consider the fact that God already knew. From Eden until now He knows. He has always known what women are, how men will cause us to struggle and what women need to do to make it.

So, what is our Father saying? He is saying that all this was necessary in order to prepare us to aspire to God not man. Our 'God in mind' mode offsets the balances and we no longer remain suspended in mid air on this circular plane earth.

Romans 8:29-30;

"For whom he did foreknow, he also did predestinate[4309]proorizó ('mark out beforehand') **conformed[4832]summorphos**('...sharing the same inner essence-identity (form); showing similar behaviour from having the same essential nature) **to the image[1504]eikón**('...properly, "mirror-like representation," referring to what is very close in resemblance (like a "high-definition"...') **of his Son, that he might be the firstborn among many brethren. Moreover whom he did predestinate, them he also called[2564]ekalesen**('I call, invite, name'): **and whom he called, them he also**

justified[1344]edikaiosen('…approve, honour, glorify…'): **and whom he justified, them he also glorified**[1392]edoxasen('to ascribe weight by recognizing real substance (value)')."

The words predestinate, conformed, called and justified in the above text are all Aorist Indicative Active 3rd Person Singular Verbs. That means they are solid and unmoveable actions which although completed in the past, are continuously, eternally active; given to us each as unique individuals. Now, reading the above scripture with proper translation we see that God picked you before you got to the planet, noted that you had the same 'stuff' inside you that He has, then invited you to the planet by name, opened up that Himness pot in you, then made preparations to explode it out of you in due time.

Wow.

2564 is 'ekalesen', which we see means 'I call, invite, name'. This is the self same word as 'church' in the scripture below, Revelation 2:1;
"Unto the angel of the church[1577]**ekklesias of Ephesus write;.."**
The only difference is that 'ekklesias' is a Genitive Feminine Singular Noun. That means it owns the preceding noun in the sentence, takes female attributes and is a singular entity.

So, stop 'going to church' every Sunday. You are wasting God's time, and your own time, not to mention the time of your brothers and sisters like me, who are patiently waiting for you to wake the hell up. You are already in the one singular Church if you are predestinated, conformed, called and justified. You now need to find those in the Body of Christ to whom you are required to assemble yourself.
Oh my God, it is the Genitive Feminine *Singular*, which meaneth that it does not necessitate that you at any time need to meet with anybody to carry out your called purpose. If you do, you do. If you don't, you don't. Will the real Church people please stand up.

As I said, stop getting up and arbitrarily gathering every Sunday, we are no longer under commandment. We are in Love; we are at Church everyday. You are Church. The Church in the above scripture owned the angel. Yes, owns the angel. Time to get busy people.

Everybody on the run in the early Church, believers from Pharisees, believers from wet believers, believers from Paul, Paul from believers, mixed believers from Pharisees, Paul from Pharisees, believers from the roman lawn mower. All the while, there was only one belief that held knowledge of God and that was real Judaism. The joudaion. The Church will always be the group who are; looking out for the wellbeing of widows and children no matter what. Best way to do that? Family groups preferably headed up by a wife and her husband.

When the husband cleaves to his wife, the curse is removed. So if we want the Floetry, the wife must be held up as first before God.

The angels need the man as first in order to minister. However, God must see the husbands present the wife first before God; totally cleaving to her, willing to die for her. No man can adjust for the physics of needing to die for a person who is currently his doormat. It will not work that way. I repeat, it will not work that way. What you will die for must be what you treasure, protect and carry before yourself the most in your life. The wife holds her husband above her before God for the sake of the ministering angels, and on the behalf of the blessings for the whole family cohort. In putting his wife first the husband in turn produces the spiritual development of Joining which comes first before the Joining of the Bride to Christ.

Then there will be no curse; back to Eden for all of us dwelling on this planet. As we saw in the joudaioi, the adversary works through people. It can't just turn up uninvited and terrorize you. In any case, Jesus took captivity captive. So, what are you waiting for?

Heaven
upon the earth

Deuteronomy 11:21

www.ingramcontent.com/pod-product-compliance
Lightning Source LLC
Chambersburg PA
CBHW070120290526
45789CB00005B/2078